D1494968

MOUNTAIN BIKE ROUTE GUIDES

SCOTLAND TRAILS

Tim Woodcock
with John Fulton

TO ONE OF THE FEW.
WHO HAVE SURVIVED.

BEST WISHES

NOV 95.

BOOKS

Dedication
For Kay, Wee John and the Coast-to-Coast crew

Author's Acknowledgements
Thanks first to the main man, John Fulton, for putting together the basic route – which he has been riding for more than a decade – then obtaining all the necessary permissions to publish it. Without his efforts this book would not have been possible.

For additional help and advices in compiling the routes: James Mackintosh and Paul Biggin of Forest Enterprise; Damien and Nick Forster of Off-Beat Bikes in Fort William; Brian Gallagher of Making Treks in Ballater.

For back-up and technical support: High Five nutrition (Karrimor Cycling Equipment); Shimano (Madison); John Mullett of Ralph Coleman Cycles, Taunton, Somerset (01823 275822).

For clothing and carrying kit: Karrimor Cycling Equipment (MTB wear and Elite/Camelbak rucksacks); Polaris (MTB clothing); Giro (helmets); John Luck (MTB boots).

For hardware: Timax (Ti MTB frames); Mavic (Ceramic MTB wheels); Halson (suspension forks), Profile (cockpit kit), Finish Line (bike care products), Park (workshop tools), all from Madison; Ritchey (pedals); Cool Tool (trail tools); WTB (tyres); Avocet (Vertech Altimeter and cycle computers).

First published in 1995 by

Future Books
a division of Future Publishing Limited
Beauford Court, 30 Monmouth Street, Bath BA1 2BW

Text and photographs copyright © Tim Woodcock 1995

Map on page 4 copyright © Estelle Corke 1995

Route maps based upon the Ordnance Survey mapping with the permission of the Controller of Her Majesty's Stationery Office © Crown Copyright

The moral right of the author has been asserted

Cover design by Maria Bowers
Edited and designed by D & N Publishing, Ramsbury, Wiltshire SN8 2HR

A CIP catalogue record for this book is available from the British Library

ISBN: 1 85981 008 X

Printed and bound by BPC Paulton Books Ltd.
A member of the British Printing Company

Reprographics by Quadcolour, Warley, West Midlands

2 4 6 8 10 9 7 5 3 1

If you would like more information on our other cycling titles please write to:
The Publisher, Future Books at the above address.

CONTENTS

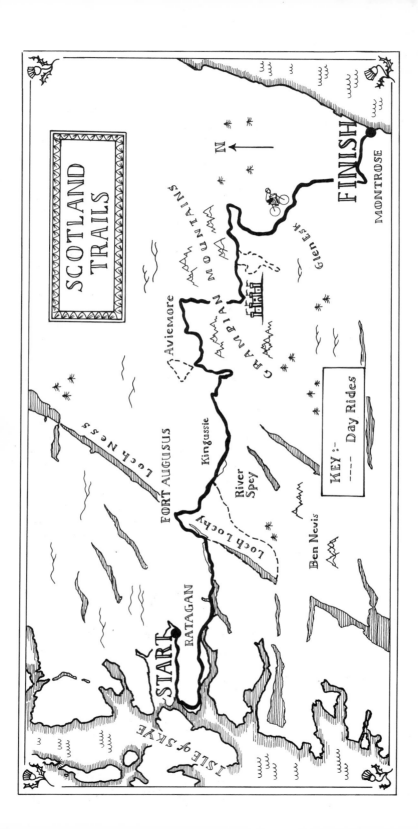

Foreword

OFF-ROAD CYCLING
A Code of Conduct for Scotland, endorsed
by *THE SCOTTISH SPORTS COUNCIL*

More people are now cycling off-road, away from busy public roads. Off-road cycling is fun, but it has its own hazards and it brings obligations. Respect the interests of land managers and owners and show courtesy to others. This code gives basic advice on access to land in Scotland, on maintaining goodwill with other users of the countryside and on safety.

ACCESS

Access to land in Scotland has long been conducted as a matter of courtesy, tolerance and goodwill. However, there is no legal right of access to land, except on a right of way or where access has been specially negotiated. By law, the off-road cyclist is entitled to use cycle-tracks and those public rights of way where a right to cycle exists under common law. The Forestry Commission provides a welcome to cyclists on its forest roads, subject to local closure for management. Many private and public owners do allow access to cyclists. Many of the traditional tracks through the glens will have right-of-way status for cycles, where use by cyclists has continued over the years, and where the route meets other tests for a right of way. Always be considerate and courteous when taking access. Ask when in doubt. Arrange events or competitions only with the consent of landowners and the guidance of the Scottish Cyclists Union. Seek consent for rallies of large groups.

THINK ABOUT OTHERS

Cycle with consideration for others, always giving way to walkers and horse riders, and to farm and forest workers. Give friendly greeting to people you approach and acknowledge the courtesy of those who give way for you. Watch your speed when close to others. Try to avoid places which are heavily used by pedestrians, especially family groups. Always dismount and walk through congested areas. Do not alarm walkers or riders by coming up silently behind them. Respect other land management activities e.g. do not pass close to forestry operations until told that it is safe to pass or disturb sheep gathering or game shooting.

CARE OF THE ENVIRONMENT

Keep to hard tracks and paths and don't short-cut corners. Walk over very soft ground to avoid cutting it up. Avoid fierce braking and skids on downhill riding to minimise damage to path surfaces. Do not take bikes onto mountain tops and plateaux where vegetation is easily damaged.

Leave the countryside as you find it. In particular, take all litter home.

LOOK AFTER YOURSELF

Take special care when cycling downhill - this is when most accidents occur. Watch your speed on loose surfaces. Match your speed to the track surface and your skills. Upland Scotland can be rough and remote. Cycle within your abilities as an accident or a breakdown in a remote place could be serious. Take a companion in remote areas. Remember that crossing burns and rivers in spate can be dangerous. Take a map and compass and know how to navigate.

Carry warm and waterproof clothing, emergency food, and a lamp. Always take tools and a puncture repair kit on long trips.

CONSIDER WEARING A HELMET AND PROTECTIVE CLOTHING.
ALSO YOUR BIKE SHOULD BE LEGAL FOR USE ON THE ROAD.

INTRODUCTION

The Ride

Riding from coast-to-coast in the Highlands is the ride of a lifetime. An epic off-road experience, the stuff of fantasy – taking on the rugged wrath of Britain's most remote mountain ranges. It's all here, between these covers, and believe me you'll not regret the day you set out to realise one of this young sport's most exhilarating dreams.

Based upon a route first explored by John Fulton, the Highland Coast-to-Coast trail sets off from Scotland's stunning Atlantic seaboard – where the windswept Western Isles muddle the meeting of land and ocean – and strikes deep into the dramatic mountainscape of the Grampians. As you climb, picturesque woodland scenes scatter; then dwindle away to isolated birch stands, bracken and heather. With height comes an awesome austerity, that quickens the pulse while you take in vistas fashioned by volcanic activity millennia past. Often you and your companions will be entirely alone, jagged peaks crowding your horizons, slate grey lochans reflecting their cerulean heights, an ancient drove road rumbling beneath your tyres. There's no better way to sample Scotland's off-road delights; but be prepared to be hooked. The Highlands have a habit of enticing the adventurous off-roader back time and time again.

The Rider

Imposing as the Highlands are, the riding is not as radical as many a newcomer to the Grampians might expect. It's a big country so there are some big climbs and, yes, there are some sections that will test the trial skills of the most ardent off-road fanatic. But for the most part a fit cyclist with an appetite to enjoy the mountain biking experience can tackle the Coast-to-Coast with confidence. Ignore the high-level routes and the ride is well within the capabilities of an MTB tyro providing they're fit for a Highland fling.

The Route

230 miles. One whole week. Seven days that kick off by refreshing that city-worn soul in the superb isolation of Kinlochourn Forest, cruising up the Great Glen above the glittering waters of Loch Oich, storming

the desolate Corrieyairack Pass then on across the heather-clad Braes of
Abernethy, through forests of Scots pine before the Highland Coast-to-
Coast cuts into the heart of the Cairngorms, up the glorious valley of
Glen Avon. Slip off the shoulders of Culardoch on a pell-mell run
down to Deeside, past the Muir of Dinnet – a tapestry of silver birch,
purple heather and dazzling lochs – to enjoy the glories of Glen Tanar
before that final climb to be conquered – Mount Keen. Scotland's most
easterly Munro dials you into the route's monster descent, then it's a
gentle road cruise to the coast to dip your tyres in the North Sea on
Montrose's sandy shore.

Off-road and macadam mileage are roughly 50/50. That might seem
a lot of tarmac but don't be a slave to mileage; on this ride you'll spend
75% of your biking in the dirt. The rest really will come as a rest.
Impatient to get stuck into the meat of the crossing, you might think
the first day too easy. Hold your horses – if you overdo it on day one
you'll find it hard to recover. Fit cyclists will find the suggested
overnights are spaced well but, should you wish to stretch or shrink
your days, there are plenty of alternatives.

Day Rides
John Fulton and I have included some day loops along the way. These
would be an ideal intro to the Big Trip or, if taking a week out to treat
yourself to the ride of a lifetime isn't feasible, cut the Coast-to-Coast up
into day ride bites and do it piecemeal.

A suspension bridge spans the giddy heights of Monessie Gorge.

BEFORE YOU GO

Fitness

There are over 500 proper mountains in Scotland, so it stands to reason that the riding should be high-level, eyeballs-out rough stuff. Wrong! And it's a common misconception. Off-road routes in the Scottish Highlands are characterised by low-level drove roads – good cart tracks that hug loch sides and only climb out of the glens when easier alternatives have run out. That said, they often sport a technical edge. Especially when they strike boldly over the braes. Not white-knuckle; 'pick a wrong line and you're dumped' technical, but an edge that demands absolute concentration. Relax for an instant during a steep ascent and grip will slip, you'll dab, stop and getting re-started can be nigh-on impossible. Often it's just your sheer determination plus a degree of dexterity with power delivery that will get you through. And that takes fitness.

But being fit is not just a question of power. It's more about recovery rate, and in the Highlands some of the climbs are big. Legs that are quick to revive are not just an asset but a necessity. Being in shape to take a mountain bike off-road in a landscape as vast and rugged as this is difficult to pick up on the trail. That's because fitness gains are made during the period of rest between spells of activity. No rest and no gain. This also means that you can't significantly increase your fitness levels in the few days before you go. You need time.

Ideally you should start getting trim at least a couple of months before the departure date. It is a long time, puts paid to travelling on a whim and the word 'preparation' rears its ugly head, but being fit will make the whole escapade more fun. For everyone. Even MTBers who get out and hit the hills regularly will benefit from some serious working out on their wheels. By the time you set off from Ratagan on the shores of Loch Duich you ought to have a few thirty-mile day loops under your belt; otherwise you'll need to slot in a couple of days furlough to allow that extra fitness to build.

Companions

Rides like this are an enriched experience if you're in good company. A well-integrated team is much better able to overcome adversities with ease;

even a simple thing like bad weather. But travelling companions are notoriously tricky to choose, and in the ups and downs betwixt beginning and end there will be stresses and strains. Long-distance off-roading is not all fun. On precipitous trails it's both difficult and demanding; add fatigue, perhaps a mis-read map and a ferocious wind and you've got a pretty good recipe for a falling out. Always distressing, discord can soon develop into dispute, and that could be dangerous in the wrong place at the wrong time. Choose companions carefully. It goes without saying that you should all get on, but don't forget fitness. One mis-match – couch potato or fitness freak – in an otherwise well-balanced band of bikers will often lead to persistent friction and cast a shadow over the whole party.

Kitting Out

HARDWARE

Travel light and ride free. Whatever you take, you've got to carry it on this trip. And when you're making height-gains in excess of 3000ft (900m) on some of the more strenuous days you'll appreciate that trimming kit to a necessary minimum makes sense. Providing you don't overdo it and skimp on essentials, saving weight is safer, too. It conserves energy and makes handling the bike on some of the more extreme terrain a lot less hairy. Heavy bikes tend to keep going when they get kicked off course! Experienced riders consider that just an extra 15lbs (7kg) in weight makes technical sections two to three times more difficult. A sobering thought!

The Wheels

I could wax lyrical about the benefits of lightweight titanium frames, tell you that suspension is a must and explain how SPDs are essential for smooth power transfer. Then tell you how to sell your mother and mortgage the house to finance the purchasing of that 'must have every-thing' trick bit and frameset. But I won't. To begin with, bike choice is a personal thing, fads and fashions change on a whim and, providing it's sound, any clunker of an MTB will do. Having said that, there are some pointers as to what makes a bike well suited to the task and what does not.

You're going to travel some steep and technical trails so use a good quality, reasonably light, proper MTB – 21 or more indexed gears – with alloy wheels, low gearing, pannier rack braze-ons, pedals with toe clips (or SPDs) and a comfortable saddle. You're looking for a bike built for comfort, not speed. One with a relatively upright position, so look for a medium length, high-rise stem, wide handlebars, and it's worth fitting bar-ends as they allow the rider to adopt a number of different riding positions. And everyone knows that a change is as good as a rest. We wish! We're talking several hundred pounds here but if you're serious about mountain biking it's worth it. Take a look at the mountain biking press for what's what then ask at a good mountain bike shop and buy the best that you can afford. If that's out of your budget then consider hiring one. Hiring is also a good way of 'balancing out' the hardware within your group. This is especially important if, for example, one of you has a clunker and the rest are riding lightweight titanium trickery decked out with suspension. On a long-distance ride, the difference in ride quality will be amplified; perhaps to the extent that it'll put a downer on the whole trip. Your bike should also be thoroughly serviced and checked out before setting off. A wheel buckle might well bring an early end to your long-awaited trip but a collapse could spell disaster, so have your wheels checked and trued before you start.

Bike Bits

Some bike accessories that should be considered essential are: bottle cages (although piggy-back drink carriers significantly reduce the likelihood of dehydration, they don't always work well with rucksacks; if you intend to use one, check it out before you go or buy one of the dedicated rucksack/drink-pack combos available); a brand new set of the best brake blocks you can afford and some branded, good quality treads, with around a 2in (5cm) carcass of new rubber for cushioning and grip. Consult a good MTB bike shop for what's the latest trend in tyres and avoid cheap 'imitations'; they're usually made with low-grade compound and won't grip as well. On this ride there's also a case for some sort of cushioning up front to negate the effects of day-on-day of riding cobbly cart track. Proper suspension is ideal, but one of the many forms of 'flex-stem' will also fend off fatigue.

May-time in the highlands. Snow-capped granite mountains, silver birch flush with spring, azure skies and not a midge in sight!

Other items to consider, especially if long-distance off-roading in Scotland really grabs you, are: an Aheadset or a headset lock-ring, Allen key crank fittings such as Crank-o-Matics, a bomb-proof set of wheels, puncture-proof tubes, top/seat tube pads to make carries more comfortable and a sprung saddle or suspension seat post. If you have SPDs check that your shoes have a deep, aggressive tread and that the cleats don't stand proud of the sole (pirouetting on a boulder on protruding cleats with a bike on your back isn't very funny). If this sounds familiar then consider re-fitting your old pedals and clips and wear walking boots instead. The loss in power transfer is minimal and the boots will offer a much firmer footing when it comes to shouldering the frameset. Some SPDs also suffer from clogging when it gets really gloopy. And it can get seriously gloopy on the eastern leg of the Highland Coast-to-Coast!

As I have a preference for keeping the bike as light as possible I didn't fit a pannier rack on this trip. Just as well because the tracks were mostly so rocky that the constant trail shock would have put a severe stress on any rack, and there were a few occasions when a pack couldn't have been safely strapped to it anyway. Having said that, there's a fair amount of tarmac, pannier racks are the next best thing to a mudguard (another item that's worth its weight in gold), and you might be glad to give your back a rest once in a while; this in exchange for sluggish bike handling at other times. Whatever you do, buy a top-quality rack – cheap ones will collapse under the constant stress of trail-shock – and preferably a hollow-tube, chromoly one.

Tools and Spares

Quality doesn't come cheap, but good tools are a godsend when you're in a fix, so be prepared to pay for them. Most multi-tools will save weight on a tool-roll of separate bits but don't forget to check that your clever widget does all the whatsits on your bike. And your companions'.

The same goes for spares. If you all run the same tyre valves, chains, straddle wires and even brake blocks, the stores can be kept to a sensible size. Once you've got all tools and spares together, pack them tight and keep them handy – ready for the inevitable trail-side emergency. The Highland Coast-to-Coast does take you over some pretty bleak and isolated scenery; even so, there's no need to go over the top with the wilderness thing and carry enough spares for a total re-build. On most days you will be within striking distance of a bike shop.

SOFTWARE

We're all aware of the weather's profound effect on our well-being – in the wet it's doom and gloom but once the sun pops out, life's a party. It's all down to environment quality and clothing dictates the quality of our immediate environment. Except clothing choice is not dictated on a whim of Nature. Kit yourself out with inappropriate gear that's been moth-balled in the wardrobe for the past five years and you're dressing up for a dose of doom and gloom. Uncomfortable. But take some time in selecting good-quality kit and you'll be pleased to face whatever the weather throws at you.

Even in summer, controlling warmth is the vital element, versatility the name of the game. Up on the Corrieyairack Pass it's a lot colder than down in Fort Augustus. You can be shivering in the icy blast of a savage hailstorm while bikers down below are sweating on the sun-warmed tracks of the Great Glen Cycle route.

Dress Sense

Kitting out a mountain biker has proved to be the outdoor clothes designers' biggest challenge yet. It's a strenuous sport, generates loads of heat at peak activity, then the loonies stand about mending punctures on a hillside with a wind-chill factor of −10°C and their body temperature plummets. But designers are rising to the challenge and there's a stack of really good, MTB-specific gear to choose from.

The multi-layer principle is bandied about as the way to go – and it works – but there's always someone who has to swim against the tide and now there are one or two manufacturers producing single-layer, pile-lined kit. This is really late winter wear but can prove ideal for weight-saving freaks and experienced bikers attempting an off-season crossing. So right from the start we're faced with a bewildering choice of kit, complicated by contrasting design convictions and all so technical that you need a science degree to discern what's what. The best approach is to decide what you want the clothing to do. For long trips its has to be light, have low bulk, be quick drying, resist the rampant sock syndrome, be easy to care for, fit well, feel comfortable and perform well. All this whether it's to wick, provide warmth, wind proofing or water resistance (you'll need clothing to perform all of these functions.). Above all, it has to let your body lose moisture and 'breathe'. Under-layer clothing that soaks up water, sags like a wet flannel and dims the lights when the tumble dryer's turned on is useless. Likewise, a top-layer that's built like a tent, flies like a kite and gives you your very own greenhouse effect is best left at home and used as a bin-liner. MTB magazines regularly review cycling kit, back-issues are easily obtainable and their advice should at least put you on the right track.

Padded biking shorts are a must. There's no other item of clothing that will do so much for so little. Cut and style vary enormously and price does not necessarily reflect comfort and quality but generally the more panels they have the better, a seamless pad is less likely to chafe and for summer biking loose-fit, touring shorts will keep you cooler. Female coast-to-coasters will find women's shorts far more comfortable than the equivalent man's version. Some folk are quite happy to bike without gloves but I invariably wipe out and grit my palms when I forget to put a pair on. Apart from protection for the accident-prone, padded mitts or gloves promote hands-on comfort levels, cushioning trail shock that would bruise you to your bones eventually. On your feet there's nothing to beat a good pair of MTB boots. That's boots, not shoes. But there are alternatives such as light walking boots and even fell-running shoes with modified soles. Both grip well and give ankle support. Don't be tempted by making do with trainers unless you're good at grass skiing with a bike on your back. Even a modest

Climbing Culardoch in the eastern Grampians. A granny-cog slog, but the gruelling climb is rewarded with a sizzling descent to Deeside.

A spectacular sunset over Loch Alsh and Skye.

grass bank can become insurmountable if your boots sport an inadequate sole. Last, but definitely not least, wear a helmet! I'm not going to tread lightly round this recommendation for fear of upsetting MTBers who want to express some notion of freedom by going bare-headed. One day you'll crack your nut and like it or not this will result in a needless call-out for the mountain rescue team.

Comfort après-trail is fundamental to your well-being. You'll want to ditch the hot dogs, sweaty shirt and humming shorts, have a shower and step into some light longs, slip on a T and put those trail-weary toes into a pair of pliable shoes. Pack-down bulk and weight is especially important with après-trail togs. They'll be on your back most of the time, so it makes sense to take trail kit that looks good off the bike.

Navigation Aids

Well you can dispense with the bulky package of maps that's the bane of most long-distance rides. They're in the back. Add to that a good-quality compass on a neck cord and weather-proof cycle computer – both of which you must be able to use with ease – and that's the pilot part sorted.

Health and Survival Gear

Mountain biking can be dangerous; a trivial accident above Kinloch Hourn or a major fall on the flanks of Mount Keen can quickly bring you down to a survival situation. A matter of life or death. Carry the right kit, make the right decisions and you can turn crisis to drama, live to tell the tale and even laugh about it. Later. A good first-aid kit and the knowledge to use it are essential. A basic kit should include antiseptic wipes, plasters, cohesive tape for wounds, triangular bandage, salt tablets for cramp, Puritabs and first aid instructions (first-aid information, covering some of the common MTB emergencies, is given on page 32). You might very well be an accomplished first-aider. Whoever comes to your aid might not and they, not to mention you, will appreciate a set of instructions ready to hand. Survival gear – mini-torch, survival bag and whistle – can all be packed with the first aid kit. Pack it in a heavy-duty, zip-tie polythene bag, label it clearly and know where it is.

Not strictly first aid but pretty important to the health department are medicaments for treating minor ailments like saddle soreness (not minor if it happens but Sudacream or E45 cream speeds recovery), athlete's foot, sun burn (which is a real hazard high up in the Highlands in spring and summer), lip chaff, muscle strain and pain and the essential midge repellent if you're cycling in summer.

In the Bag

You'll encounter hill walkers from time to time as parts of the Coast-to-Coast ride and popular walking routes share the trail – especially in the east – and many of them will be strolling along with pint-sized day-packs to take their kit. Take a leaf out of their book. Travel light and leave it on your back.

A small rucksack – about 30l capacity – together with either a bumbag, small seat pack or bar bag should be fine. Features to look for on a rucksack are a narrow profile, light weight, waist and chest security straps, wide shoulder straps (easily adjusted and locked), compression straps and a low pack height (try it out, packed full, with your helmet on. Look straight up and if the helmet is knocked forwards over your eyes then that's what will happen on the bike). Such features can often be found on climbing and fell-running backpacks but there are MTB-specific rucksacks and there are some that can be swapped from back to a pannier rack and back with ease.

If you have problems packing all your kit into thirty-odd litres of space then try rolling the clothes into tight cylinders, holding them down and tying with compression straps (Velcro straps are ideal). Remember to put the least dense gear at the bottom, the heaviest at the top and ensure the back-panel is comfortable against your spine.

Scotland Trails Kit List

A handy, pre-'flight' check list is provided but don't regard it as definitive – I habitually carry a pair of mini-Molegrips, half a toothbrush and a pair of earplugs on these trips. I'll leave you to fathom out why. Lists are an important aid to successful trip planning – a finely honed trip-list is one of the most valuable bits of kit you'll ever use – and making your own will encourage you to evaluate each item on its merits. Try this for starters:

 **KIT**

TOOL KIT
Pump
Tyre levers
Full set of Allen keys
Small, adjustable wrench
Screwdriver (cross-head and flat)
Chain-splitter
Spoke key
Penknife

BIKE SPARES
Inner tube
Puncture repair kit
Brake blocks
Straddle wire
Lube
Rear gear cable
Rear light/batteries
Cable ties
Allen bolts for bottle cages etc
Gaffer/carpet tape

Couple of spare chain links
Cable lock
Water bottle(s)

CYCLE CLOTHING
Padded shorts (2 pairs min.)
Sports socks (3 pairs min.)
Cool shirt, short-sleeved
Cycle shirt, long-sleeved
Wicking/thermal top
Padded bike mitts
Helmet (not extreme, elongated, aero-type)
Fleece/mid-layer top
Windproof top
Waterproof top with hood
Tights or windproof over-trousers
MTB Boots

APRÈS TRAIL
Light-weight longs
Underwear
Shorts
Baseball boots/sandals or similar

PERSONAL KIT
Wash kit inc. small, quick-drying towel
Zipped wallet with money
Plastic
SYHA card/B&B contacts
Pencil
Sewing kit (polyester thread)
Medical kit
Head torch/batteries

TRAIL KIT
Compass
Computer
First-aid kit
Survival kit (whistle, bag, torch)
Emergency food (cereal bars, etc.)
Rucksack with liner
Seat pack and/or Bar/bumbag (to keep emergency kit separated)

If you're expecting cold, wet weather then you'll need to add extra clothing, especially thermals (tights, tops and socks), full gloves, headband/snood and waterproof socks. In winter an extra-warm fleece/windproof top, for when you're caught in the open with an emergency repair, lined mitts and lined hood will also be necessary if you're tackling the high-level routes. On the hardware side, don't forget lights – you may be caught out in the dark.

How heavy will this lot weigh? For a summer crossing aim for about 5.5–6.5kg (12–14lb) for all your personal kit and about 3kg (7lb) of shared gear (including food). With three up you'll each have about 7.5kg (16lb) of kit on board.

Accommodation

From the first, one of the key considerations is where you are going to sleep. Even how you are going to sleep. Comfort and a good night's rest are keynotes to the success of long-distance cycling and only you will know what your absolute needs are. Consider them carefully – you owe it to yourself.

Camping

Camping and self-sufficiency seem to go hand-in-hand with the adventure of mountain biking but – and it's a big but – the penalties are high. First of all, it is an offence in Scotland to camp or light fires on private land without the consent of the owner. All land is 'owned' by someone, so your first task should be to get permission, though landowners are usually tolerant of careful campers. Then the tent, stove, sleeping bag, mat, cooking kit and food, plus additional clothes and the out-sized rucksack to put it all in will weigh you down by an extra stone or so, and can make technical trail riding ridiculously difficult. Descents are interesting though, if lethal! Survivors, exhausted by a day beneath their burden, will then have the pleasure of finding a pitch, setting the tent, searching out a stream, fetching the water and washing cold. Then it's cook, eat, clean-up and finally fall into a stupor only to be driven spare at first light – which is extremely early in Scotland in summer – by a demented bunch of birds doing their dawn chorus thing! Camping's great.

Aqua-mode in Abernethy Forest. John Fulton splashes with panache but bikers beware, bigger burns lie ahead.

Bed and Breakfast

By way of comparison, at the opposite extreme, we have B&Bs. First and foremost, you can dump all that camping kit and ride light. Not day-ride light but nimble enough to loft wheels, bunny hop and skip the rear end round the odd rock. And that's handy. It's fun too! Add to that an end-of-day cuppa followed by a hot bath, supper in the pub, uninterrupted sleep, a breakfast to build a day's trail blazing on and the pleasure of being the guests of some of the best hosts one could wish for and you've got luxury. But it costs and, in season, pre-booking is advisable. That means some sort of timetable.

SYHAs and Private Hostels

Somewhere between the two above alternatives are hostels. You need only carry the same kit as for B&Bs and they're much cheaper. Most provide a full range of services – from shop to showers in the case of

SYHAs – and if you're not the self-catering type some private hostels can even provide an evening meal; check when you book. Add to that a good drying room and you can see hostels are handy. On the downside, mucking in with a bunch of strangers night after night isn't always ideal, accommodation is single-sex, in dormitories, and sharing a hostel with a bunch of hyper-active juveniles still trying to fight their way free of the education system is not fun! But, all in all, hostels are the best bet and trail-weary bikers are usually well catered for.

The Scottish Highlands have a fair few hostels and the Highland Coast-to-Coast has five SYHAs along its length together with three or four private hostels. Most are conveniently located so that you can hostel-hop along the entire route though the leap from Ballater to the coast is quite a haul. All the hostels are listed separately (see page 95). Pre-booking is prudent in high-season and be warned – those jolly school parties are a maverick in the accommodation calendar at any time. Many hostels, like B&Bs, have a closed season so the accommodation logistics of a winter crossing need more careful planning.

Bothies and Bunkhouses

Bothies were originally provided for itinerant workers and are traditional, single-storey shelters which often look like isolated, abandoned cottages. These days, individual estates or the Mountain Bothies Association maintains them for the use of hillgoers and, as they're provided for passers-by, they are almost always unlocked. The principle of casual occupation relies upon responsible and caring use, and traditionally visitors leave an item of non-perishable food or drink for those that follow. Unfortunately, recent years have seen a marked increase in vandalism and abuse of these 'community' shelters which has lead to some being locked or left to go to ruin, so bothies vary greatly in quality.

Bunkhouses are budget accommodation usually associated with a hotel and so are often a bit less rude than a bothy. If you are going to rely on bothies and bunkhouses for accommodation, think of them more as stone tents and kit yourself out appropriately. Popular ones can get crowded; bothies and bunkhouses fall out of use so it would be wise to check with the appropriate hotel or estate before you plan your itinerary. Estate addresses can be found in the book *Heading For The Hills* published by the Scottish Mountaineering Trust.

HIGHLAND BOUND

When to Go

The midges in Scotland have a legendary reputation that's justly deserved. Try fixing a flat when there's a swarm of those voracious little vermin impaling every inch of exposed flesh with a million itchy nips! And nobody's going to hang about and lend you a hand – not after the first time! The midge season runs from June to September but, if you have to go then, take solace from the fact that a slight breeze grounds the little blighters. Just keep riding. Midges aside, there's no doubt that late spring sees Scotland's best weather, plus the days are blessed with long, drawn-out evening light and the Highlands in autumn are astoundingly beautiful though the weather at that time varies from one extreme to another.

Getting There

The great thing about The Highland Coast-to-Coast is that it begins and ends with convenient rail access which means you don't have to bring the car. At the western end Kyle of Lochalsh is the Scot Rail terminus for the Highlands and Islands and has a regular rail service running three trains per day, Monday through Saturday which can carry up to four bikes each. If you're setting off from Ratagan bear in mind that you'll have a 17m (27km) cycle ride round the coast from Kyle. Montrose, at the eastern end, is on an Inter-City line with excellent services to the rest of the country. There's the usual cyclist levy so the key rule is to check and re-check, and booking is essential. Scot Rail Info has a local rate line on 0345 212282.

Car-born Sassenachs are advised to use the good old A74/M74 combo up from Gretna, pick up the M73/M8/Glasgow/Erskine Bridge route to the A82 then follow that through Fort William to Invergarry in the Great Glen to pick up the A87 to Shiel Bridge where a minor road takes you along the coast to Ratagan.

Loch Duich, described as Scotland's most beautiful sea loch, is the setting for the start of the Scotland Trail (overleaf).

ON THE RIDE

Off the Road

Ride safe. Ride light. Being the new boys on the block, mountain bikers have run the gauntlet of being alienated by other countryside users since the word go but the sport of mountain biking is flourishing. Road improvements have dramatically shrunk the distance, separating metropolis from previously isolated moor and mountain, so our wilderness areas have witnessed a motorised invasion of leisure seekers. For a time hikers (and to a lesser extent, hackers) had it pretty much to themselves but today increasing numbers have found that cycling intensifies their enjoyment of the countryside. A rump of ramblers see us as rivals, ill-informed environmentalists call us erosionists and some farmers fear that speeding bikes will frighten stock and uncaring cyclists will flatten crops.

The fact that it's a re-run of early rambler versus landowner conflicts makes no difference. Neither does the fact that the hoary chestnuts of 'tyres tear up trails' and 'bikers are the beasts of the bridleways' are perceived, not proven, concerns of some of our countryside companions. But we're here to stay; entrenched attitudes are already changing and this will come about more quickly if we ride responsibly.

Access, Trespass and Rights of Way

Although we have taken every care to try and ensure that the mapped Highland Coast-to-Coast route and the subsidiary Day Loops will keep your cycling within the law, at the very least the status of some sections is likely to change. Plus, of course, you may get lost, so it is as well to be sure of your rights.

Visitors to Scotland may be surprised to learn that there is no law against trespass but trespassers – folk who access private land without the landowner's consent – may be asked to leave and evicted using reasonable force if necessary. And remember, all land is owned by someone – even the remote mountain areas on this route – and you must take care not to cause any damage. Trespassers causing damage or nuisance may be prosecuted, subject to proof of the offence. If a landowner asks that you leave it is in your best interests, no matter what the right and wrong of it may be, to acquiesce.

On private land we have a legal right to use recognised Rights of Way which may be anything from a tarmac road no different from a public highway to a faint 'sheep' path across a mountain. Most of the routes in this book follow Rights of Way. But the law in Scotland has muddied the water with two conflicting statutes; a ruling in 1930 specifically states that a bicycle may be used on any pedestrian Right of Way and the 1984 Roads (Scotland) Act makes it an offence to cycle on a footpath without permission. In practice, cycling is allowed on Rights of Way be they track or path but elsewhere much depends upon the co-operation between landowner and cyclist which is why we are able to use many tracks and paths where there is no legal right. Some of the routes in this book are along permissive tracks and paths. Cycling is not permitted on open land.

Of course you may be bowling along a Public Right of Way when up pops a barbed wire fence and the way is blocked. It's a tricky situation because your rights are wrapped in a woolly bit of rhetoric which says you can remove the obstacle sufficiently to get past if it is reasonably possible or make a short detour to get round it. But remember that the landowner can prosecute if you cause any damage so clambering over it – often the instinctive reaction – is not a clever thing to do. Rights of Way rarely get blocked but if you're forced to detour around an obstruction report it to the Scottish Rights of Way Society (the address and details of membership is given on page 96) who will take up the matter on your behalf.

Codes of Conduct

In following the Highland Coast-to-Coast off-road route you will be treading in the tyre tracks of others. If they've careered along, forged furrows across the heather, stampeded deer, left gates gaping and created a trail of havoc and mayhem then you're not going to get a warm reception from the countryside community. Nor is anybody else who follows along unless you follow the Country and Off-road Codes.

They're not really a set of rules so much as guidelines that any responsible, thoughtful member of the mountain biking community would adopt without a second's thought. It is also strongly recom-mended that you do not take a dog; a landowner is legally entitled to destroy a dog which is considered a threat to livestock. Apart from that, you'll run even the fittest hound off its feet.

Highland Activities

Many of the estates generate their income from grouse shooting, red deer stalking, forestry and sheep farming. Visitors should be aware that these operations are subject to seasonal fluctuations in activity.

Red Deer Stalking	1st July to 15th February (15th August to 15th October is usually the period of most activity).
Grouse Shooting	12th August to 10th December (August to October is usually the busiest).
Lambing	Mid-April to June depending on location.
Logging	Any time but February, May and June are favoured 'dry' months.

It can be seen that mid-August to mid-October is a critical period and best avoided but if you have to ride in the height of the season, please make sure you use and stick to Rights of Way and I strongly recommend that you contact the stalkers on the relevant estates before you go. Addresses can be found in the book *Heading For The Hills* published by the Scottish Mountaineering Trust. Apart from alerting you to the estate operations which may conflict with your visit, stalkers are a valuable source of information as to the state of the trail, bridges, fords and snow cover.

Sandy tracks snake their way through an amber ocean of heather.

Take heed of the warning sign! It's the toughest, rideable climb of the crossing with an intimidating reputation. The Corrieyairack Pass starts here.

Ride Safety

Three's company, not two, and four's fine outdoors in the wilds. In the event of one getting badly injured someone can go for help and someone can stay with the casualty. But ideally two should go for help, not one, which is why four is better. Any more and mountain bikers in a bunch can be an intimidating party on a narrow path.

Abilities, strength and stamina in any group will vary. Keep within the capacity of everyone, watch your pace and make sure everyone keeps within sight and sound of each other. But don't bunch up, especially on downhills and along technical sections, or there'll be some rear-end wipe-outs. And they can be really nasty! It's always a good idea to wait for stragglers at the top of climbs, at the bottom of tricky descents, at wide fords and at gates. It's in the nature of a strung-out group to separate even further at such points so make sure that the young, eager pup out in front is aware of it.

One of the first signs of fatigue is when your normally ebullient companion rides quiet and persistently lags behind. Don't push it. Rest, drink, eat and keep warm – exposure may be just around the corner. Prevention is better than cure. Eat heartily at supper and breakfast, eat lots of carbohydrates, make full use of the various sports recovery drinks and carbo-loading preparations now available – after all you're just as deserving of their benefits as the athletes who advertise the stuff – and make sure you 're-fuel' within an hour or so of arriving at your overnight stop. Try not to ride for more than an hour without having some food – not as easy as it sounds – and drink regularly and drink plenty, before you get thirsty. Mountain streams are a valuable source of clean drinking water for the long-distance wayfarer so there's often no need to set off with a full day's supply – just top up along the way. To enjoy the luxury of a flavoured re-fill, take a clean plastic bag dosed with your favourite drink powder and always take your water upstream of a crossing and from a place where the water is swift flowing. Don't be over-confident when assessing how much of the Highland Coast-to-Coast should pass under your tyres during the day. Even the terminally fit will find that forty miles (sixty kilometres) is about as far as they want to go in one day. Always wear enough to keep warm and, if you stop in cold weather, put an extra layer on.

River Crossing

There are many remote river crossings on the Highland Coast-to-Coast and though many have footbridges, many do not. All the fords along the route are easily crossed during periods of dry weather but never underestimate the dangers involved in fording rivers. Here are a few pointers for ford crossing.

Safety is of paramount importance so firstly don't be so pre-occupied with trying to keep your feet dry that you end up rock-hopping upstream of a set of rapids, bike on your back where one slip may send you skidding into wild water. Take your time to select a good crossing point. Choose a shallow stretch of water that you can easily wade across – no more than knee-deep; often this is where it widens out, has many small standing wavelets and the appearance of a 'babbling brook'. Keep well clear of unruffled, dark, narrower stretches – they are likely to be deep – and of big standing waves created by water rushing over large rocks or an uneven bed. White, noisy water is also a real no-no. If you're unsure then don't attempt to cross. Don't carry your bike, use it as a prop, face upstream and if it looks at all tricky don't all cross at once. If you are forced to use step-stones it's a good idea to go across sans-frameset, select the firmest footing then return with the wheels. Again the bike is best used as a prop if your footing is insecure and sometimes it's best to take your boots off. SPD cleats that stand proud of the sole can be very slippery – unnerving!

Weather

Out in the wilds, weather will make or break a day. In western Scotland and the Grampian Mountains the elements are notoriously changeable and in the Highlands it's all in a day's weather to experience sun, sleet, rain, wind, warmth, cold and calm. Maybe the Highlands are minor mountains on the world map but it can be as bleak as Arctic tundra up amongst the hills and braes when winter gets a grip. Don't set out ill-informed and unprepared and end up the subject of a mountain rescue operation. Get the most recent weather forecast – telephone numbers are given on page 95 – and make a habit of catching the latest TV weather forecasts. They give a useful overview of what's coming.

Three factors that strangers to the mountains often fail to take into account are altitude, wind and winter. As you climb, temperature falls. Roughly speaking temperature falls one centigrade degree for every 100m gain in height (3°C per 1000ft) on a clear day, half that drop on a cloudy one. Wind-chill – the extra cooling effect as a result of body heat being robbed by the wind – increases with wind strength. In a gentle to moderate breeze (force 3, about 10mph) wind-chill is about –5°C, about –10°C in a fresh, gusty breeze (force 5, about 20mph) and –15°C in a really strong wind (force 7, about 30mph). For example on a clear, calm day the temperature on the Corrieyairack Pass will be about 7°C colder than in Fort Augustus which is some 2500ft (750m) lower. Add in the cooling effect of the inevitable wind that whips across this col, say a brisk breeze, and up on the Pass, temperatures will dip a chilling 14°C or so! Even in summer, temperature frequently falls to 5°C, in mid-winter we're talking down another 10–14°C. That's way below zero, so no wonder this route is officially tagged as being alpine/Arctic between November and March! Makes you think, doesn't it?

It would be foolish to take on high-level sections of the Coast-to-Coast if gale force winds are forecast, knowing that they'll be more ferocious on the tops. Take a furlough and live to bike another day or use one of the low-level alternatives. And be prepared to take an unplanned detour if the weather deteriorates badly whilst you're out. This is all the more likely if there's a river to ford. There's precious little soil to soak up a heavy downpour and innocuous streams may rise rapidly to become boiling torrents; rivulets to raging rivers in minutes! This is especially true in the spring when snow melt has already water-logged the ground. Forecasts give temperatures but it's as well to bear in mind, when planning a departure date, that winter temperatures will be 10–15°C colder than summer ones. Nippy!

Then, of course, there's snow. Snow-covered mountain tracks often disappear under a white blanket beneath which lurks a mountain biker's minefield. Moderate descents turn into treacherous toboggan runs, creeping streams create thick slick sheets of ice, innocuous drifts cover wheel-grabbing gullies and a few inches of slush 'n' stuff can quickly reduce your progress to a very pedestrian push. The effort factor can leap fourfold! Add a white-out where visibility is reduced to your bar-ends and we're in trouble. And don't think we're talking mid-winter here. Snow will be encountered between November and April though sometimes it kicks in by mid-October and lingers on into May. There are many fatal accidents in Scotland – some along this route and not just in winter. The Highlands demand a respect not normally associated with off-roading in other parts of Britain.

Lost?

Navigation can be tricky. Keeping on course depends on you, and preferably your companions as well, knowing your position at *all* times. Danger zones are forests, open moor and at times of poor visibility, so take care to read the terrain correctly in these situations and make no assumptions about this or that trail being a 'main' route. One way of coping with poor visibility is to follow a compass bearing to the most distant visible marker (not a sheep because it might walk off!), cycle to it, take another bearing on the next marker, cycle and so on. With very few exceptions, you'll be riding on obvious tracks so you are more likely to feel lost than really be lost.

A sight for train trekkers to Ratagan – Eilean Donan castle at the mouth of Loch Duich is an American's dream come true.

But, despite our best endeavours to keep you on track, there's always a chance you might wander from the route. Nobody intends to get lost and it comes as a shock. Don't panic. Stop. Make sure everybody's with you and then try to work out where you went wrong. Not too far back you'll have been sure of your position. Find it on the map. Naturally you'll have been using your cycle computer to keep a log of point-to-point distances and it's a simple matter of reading the distance off, calculating direction and that'll give you an approximate position. Forgotten to zero the trip distance at the last known point? Then estimate how long ago you were there and in which direction you have travelled during the elapsed time. Allowing for ground conditions, calculate how far you've cycled. Now check your surroundings and see if local landmarks coincide with your findings. If you're still unsure and visibility is poor then stay put until conditions improve.

In an ideal world three distinct landmarks should be recognised for you to be absolutely certain of your locality though, given two, you can still take compass bearings to position yourself. It goes without saying that correct use of the compass and trusting it, not your instincts, is vital.

Accident Procedure

It's vital that at least one of the party is a qualified first-aider. Ideally all of you should know the fundamentals of first aid. The British Red Cross, St John Ambulance and St Andrew's Ambulance Societies all run courses so, if you haven't done already, book into one. One day, somebody will thank you for it.

It can't be over-emphasised that carrying a proper first aid kit with instructions and being a competent first aider is an essential part of accident procedure. But first aid instructions don't always cover the common illness and injuries associated with wild country mountain biking. These are given below:

Hypothermia

(exposure – the most common cause for rescue calls)

SYMPTOMS:
Complaints of fatigue; cold, visual abnormalities; lethargy, lack of interest; cold, clammy skin, pale in colour; slurred speech; cramps; clumsiness; odd behaviour; out-of-character actions; collapse and coma. Assume exposure if two or more of these symptoms are apparent and treat immediately.

ACTION:
Stop. Do not continue in the hope that you'll find shelter. **Shelter the**

patient. Wrap them in extra clothing and put them in the survival bag, with someone else if possible. If you have a sleeping bag then use it as an inner layer. **Warm the patient** with bodily companionship and a warm drink if possible. Easily digested energy food can be given provided the patient is not too drowsy. **Cheer the patient up** – low morale is a contributory factor. Be positive – the rest of the group will be feeling pretty worried. **Rest the patient** for a prolonged period. If there's any doubt about the patient's ability to recover then send for help. **Look for signs of exposure** in other members of the party and signs of frostbite if conditions are severe. **Do not rub** the patient to restore circulation. **Do not give alcohol** – it may cause collapse.

In extreme cases, patients sometimes stop breathing so be prepared to give mouth-to-mouth, if the patient does lose consciousness place them in the recovery position. **Seek Medical Help.**

Heat Exhaustion

(common during periods of sustained effort)
SYMPTOMS:
Pale, sweaty skin; complaints of dizziness, fatigue and headache; cramps; rapid but weak pulse; shallow breathing; fainting.
ACTION:
Shade the patient. Find a cool, shady spot and lie them down. **Cold drinks of water**, slightly salted and with a little sugar if possible, will soon aid recovery. **Seek Medical Help.**

Heatstroke

(severe heat exhaustion)
SYMPTOMS:
Restlessness; frequent passing of urine; complaints of dizziness and headache; hot, flushed, dry skin; rapid, strong pulse; fainting.
ACTION:
Cool the patient by placing them in shade and remove their clothing. **Sponge their body** with water until their body temperature drops and they appear to recover. **Seek Medical Help Immediately.**

Shock

(present in almost all cases of traumatic accidents)
SYMPTOMS:
Pale and pallid skin, especially the lips; rapid, weak pulse; rapid, shallow breathing; cold, sweaty skin; complaints of dizziness and blurred vision; restlessness; yawning, pronounced sighing; fainting.
ACTION:
Reassure the patient. External bleeding or other injuries should be treated simultaneously. **Lie the patient down**, protected from the ground and elements if it is cold, avoiding unnecessary movement. **Turn their head to one side. Raise their feet** on a pile of clothes or small rucksack. **Loosen restrictive clothing. Control Body Temperature** with loose clothing. **Do not give food or drink. Do not apply heat** from an artificial source. **Seek Medical Help Immediately.**

Dislocation

(elbow, shoulder and knee joints are most at risk)

SYMPTOMS:

Deformity of the joint, especially when compared to the joint on the opposite side of the body; swelling around the joint; lack of mobility; severe pain associated with the joint.

ACTION:

Support the injured limb in a comfortable position.

Use the triangular bandage for arm/shoulder dislocations when the patient can sit or stand, rolled-up clothes for the leg. **Do not try** to manipulate the joint. **Do not move** the affected joint unnecessarily. **Seek Medical Help.**

Broken Collar Bone

(Perhaps the most common MTB fracture)

SYMPTOMS:

Patient supports injured arm against the body; head inclined towards the injured shoulder; lack of mobility in the injured side; swelling at the front of injured shoulder.

ACTION:

Position arm of injured side with fingers up towards the opposite shoulder, palm flat against the body, so far as the patient will allow. Place soft padding between the upper arm and body. Support the arm using the triangular bandage for an elevation sling off the good shoulder that encloses the elbow, forearm and hand. **Secure the arm** against the body with a belt or rucksack strap that encircles the body. **Do not move the injured arm** if it is too painful, support against the body *in situ*. **Seek Medical Help.**

Caledonian Canal cruising on the Great Glen Cycle Route. An ideal intro to Highland riding.

MAP 1

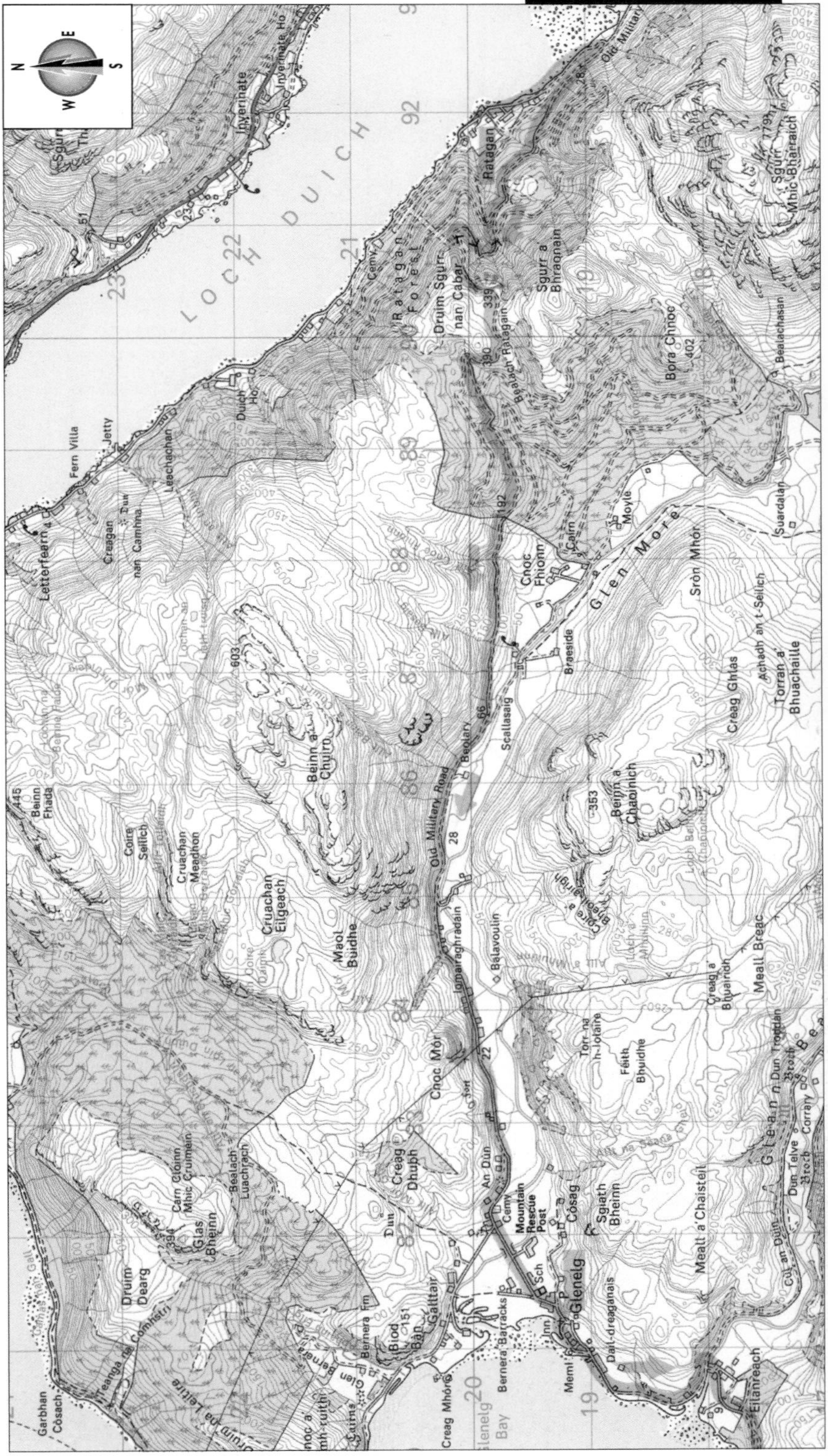

LOCH DUICH
Ratagan Forest
Ratagan
Druim Sgurr nan Cabar
Sgurr a Bhragnain
Bealach Ratagain
Bora Chnoc
Bealachasan
Sgurr Mhic Bharraich
Invérinate
Letterfearn
Fern Villa
Jetty
Duich Ho
Leachachan
Creagan Dubh nan Camhna
Beinn Fhada
Coire Seillich
Cruachan Meadhon
Cruachan Eilgeach
Maol Buidhe
Beinn a' Chuirn
Old Military Road
Beolary
Scallasaig
Braeside
Choc Fhionn
Cairn
Moyle
Glen More
Sròn Mhòr
Suardalan
Achadh an t-Seilich
Torran a' Bhuachaille
Creag Ghlas
Beinn a' Chaoinich
Meall Breac
Creag a' Bhuainidh
Torr na h-Iolaire
Féith Bhuidhe
Choc Mòr
Balavoulin
Iomairaghradain
An Dùn
Creag Dhubh
Dun
Cosag
Sgiath Bheinn
Mountain Rescue Post
Glenelg
Dail-dreaganais
Meall a' Chaisteil
Gleann Beag
Dun Troddan Broch
Dun Telve Broch
Corrary
Càl an Dùin
Eilanreach
Bernera Barracks
Bernera Fm
Biod Bàn
Galltair
Creag Mhòr
Glenelg Bay
Glas Bheinn
Carn Cloinn Mhic Cruimein
Bealach Luachrach
Druim Dearg
Garbhan Cosach
Teanga na Comhstri
Druim na Leitire
Inn
Sch

MAP SECTION

ROUTE ABBREVIATIONS AND INSTRUCTIONS

The route is split into seven days of riding, but this is only a guideline. The highlighted villages and landmarks on the maps correspond to key points in the route directions. A brief description of the day's ride, including parts of the route to watch out for, is provided at the beginning of each day's ride. Overnight stops are suggested but again only as a guideline.

The instructions are brief and to the point to make them easy to follow while riding. If in any doubt, always refer to the map and check your compass to ensure you are heading in the right direction. Compass directions are given after each turning.
The following abbreviations have been used:

Turn L : Turn left
Turn R: Turn right
SO: Straight on

KEY

 Map Orientation

 Technical Information

 Overnight Stops

 Off-Road Code

 Wet Weather Route

 Bike Care

NOTE TO THE MAP SECTION:

The maps used are based upon the Ordnance Survey 1:50 000 series which have been reduced by 20%. Therefore, one mile is equivalent to one inch and one kilometre to 1.6 cm.

Kilometres:

| 1 km | 2 km |

Statute miles:

| 1 m | 2 m |

<u>DAY 1</u> Maps 1 – 3

RATAGAN TO ARNISDALE
19m (30km), no off-road cycling; 2500ft (760m) climbing.
Summits and passes: Bealach Ratagain 1300ft (399m); Uranan Viewpoint 690ft (208m).

Set right on the shore of Loch Duich and in the shadow of the Five Sisters of Kintail, Ratagan is an ideal place to start. Though this leg is all on road it's pretty quiet, singletrack for the most part with stunning views over the sea to Skye and the Western Isles. The coastal scenery imparts a real sense of quitting the Atlantic shore. Inland, the mountains dominate the horizon. A sight to quicken the pulse and heighten the sense of anticipation.

Some pre-ride stretching is recommended – the first climb is an intimidating 1100ft (340m) over Bealach Ratagain. Pick a low gear and take it slowly and, as the views open out over Kintail Forest behind you, take ten and take in the views. With by far the biggest height gain in the bag there's a manic, tyre-skip descent to follow as you fly down into Glen More (here you can detour up Glen More then down Gleann Beag to take in some gratuitous off-road on the excuse of visiting three of the finest Brochs – Iron Age forts – in spectacular settings) to meet the coast at Glenelg. From here, the little road roller-coasts its way to Arnisdale on the shores of Loch Hourn, Scotland's most inaccessible and spectacular sea loch.

LOCATION   ROUTE DIRECTIONS

RATAGAN

Start Ratagan SYHA (GR 919199) by Loch Duich. Turn L (SE) for 1m (1.6km) to T-junction with C-road then turn R (NW) for 18m (29km) – starting with big climb, keeping SO at junctions, passing

GLENELG

through Glenelg (**accommodation available**) and Arnisdale (**accommodation available – recommended 1st night**) – to T-junction with track to Glenfield (0.5m/0.8km beyond Arnisdale chapel).

OFF-ROAD CODE
● **Enjoy the countryside and respect its life and work**

MAP 2

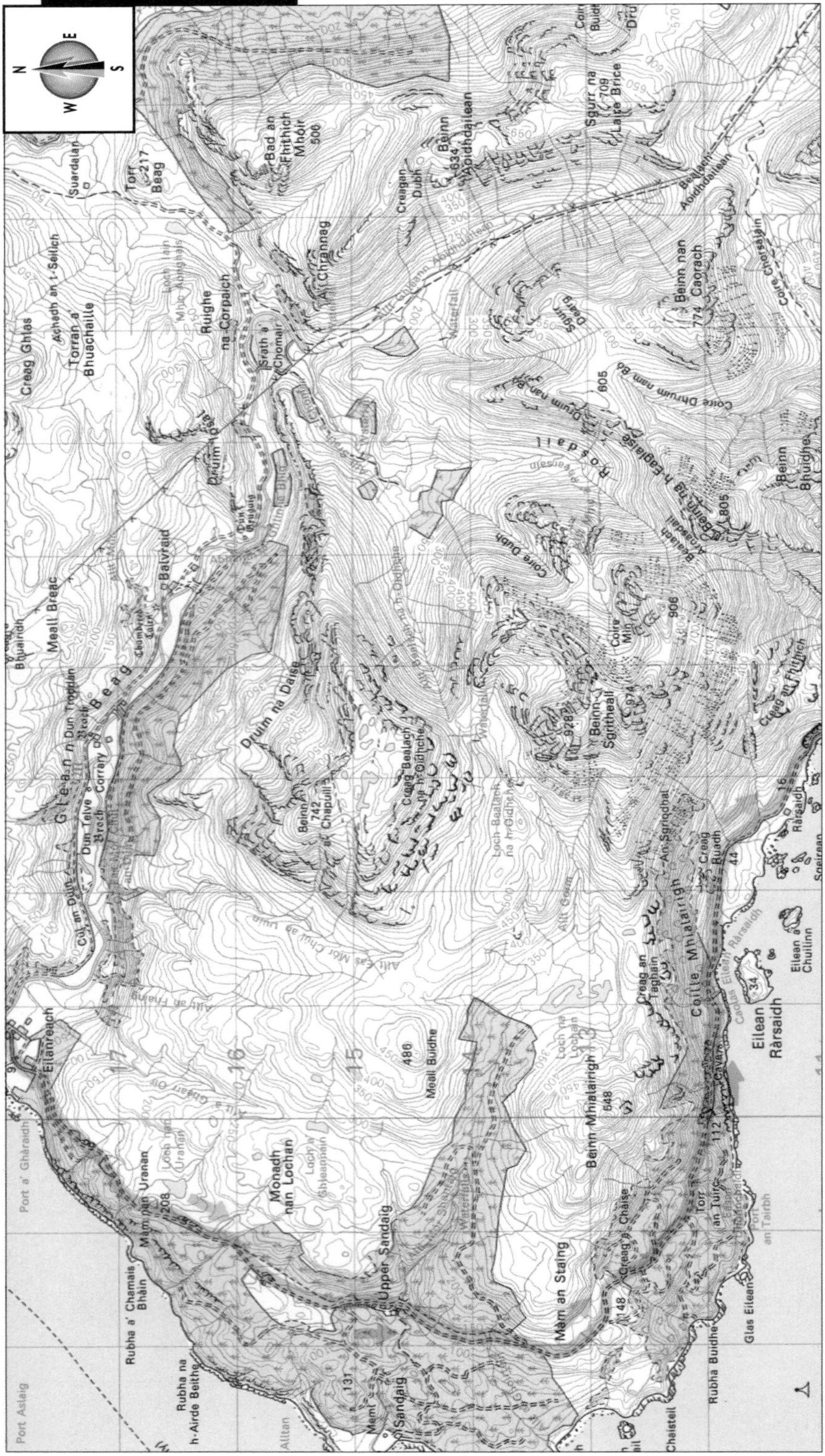

N E S W

Creag Ghlas
Achadh an t-Seilich
Torran a' Bhuachaille
Suardalan
Torr
Beag
Bad an
Fhithich Mhòir
Creagan
Dubh
Beinn
Aondhallean
Sgurr na
Làire Brice
Mullach an Achaidh Mhòir
Allt Chrannag
Rìghe
na Corpaich
Srath a'
Chomair
Druim Odhar
Beinn nan
Caorach
Coire Dhruim nam Bà
Meall Breac
Beag
Gl e a n n
Dun Troddan
Corrary
Druim na Daise
Rossail
Druim nan Bò
Bhuairidh
Dun Telve
Cùl an Dùin
Leitir
Cùil Dhoireach
Creag Bealach
na h-Oidhche
Loch Bealach
na h-Oidhche
Coire Dubh
Beinn
Sgritheall
Coire Min
Creag na Faoilinn
Allt Mòr Chùl an Dùin
Allt na Léigheadh
486
Meall Buidhe
Loch na
Lochan
Creag an
Fheadain
Creag na Fuirich
An Sgorrdhail
Creag
Ruadh
Coille Mhialairigh
Eilean
Ràrsaidh
Eilean a'
Chuilinn
Eilanreach
Mam an Uranan
208
Monadh
nan Lochan
Loch a'
Ghleannain
Beinn Mhialairigh
648
Waterfalls
Torr
an Tuill
112
Caolas Ràrsaidh
Rubha a' Chamais
Bhàin
Upper Sandaig
Màm an Staing
Creag a' Chaise
Port
an Taoibh
Rubha na
h-Airde Beithe
131
Mam
Sandaig
48
Torr
an Tuill
Rubha Buidhe
Chaisteil
Glas Eilean
Port Aslaig
Alltan

MAP 3

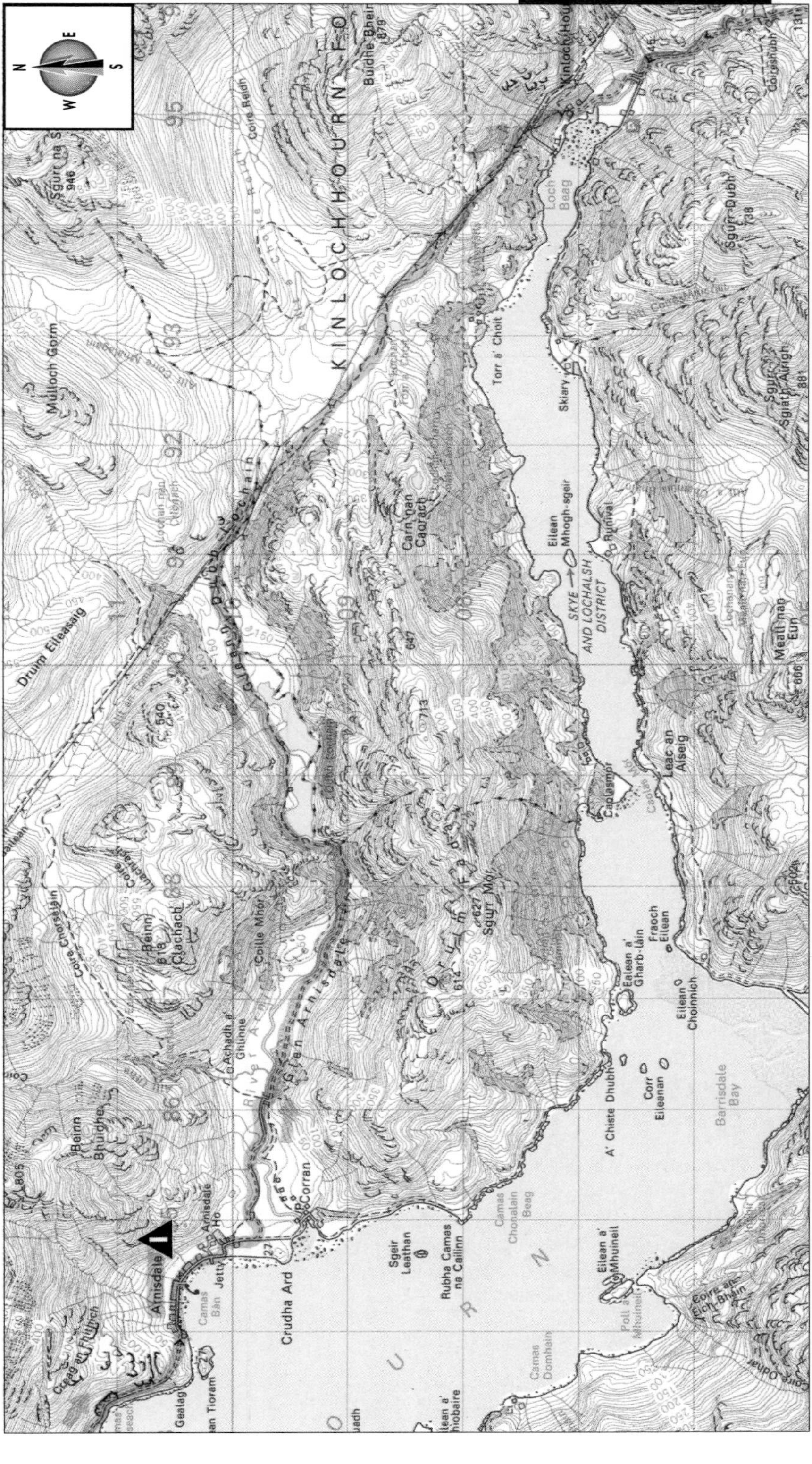

MAP 3–8

DAU 2 Maps 3 – 8

ARNISDALE TO FORT AUGUSTUS
42m (67km), 21m (34km) off-road; 3200ft (970m) climbing.
Summits and passes: Gleann Dubh Lochain 790ft (240m); Cadha Mor 800ft (245m); Choire Pass 690ft (209m); Glengarry Forest 695ft (210m); Invergarry 450ft (137m).

This is a big day, so take it steady right from the start. It's straight into off-road with a vengeance. With mountains crowding the horizon, some soaring well over 2000ft (700m), it's surprising that the gentle intro up Glen Arnisdale lasts as long as it does. The heights quickly enclose the valley and suddenly you're faced with an extraordinary climb – a push for the most part – away from the river and up onto technical singletrack through the trees.

This sets the tone for some scintillating semi-technical riding, surrounded by majestic mountain scenery. Now you really know you've embarked on a remarkable journey. Off-road right across the Highlands of Scotland. After climbing across the col of Cadha Mor you're in for some well-deserved downhilling into Kinloch Hourn spiced up with random rocks, steps and ruts to round off some pretty amazing mountain biking.

From here on navigation is straightforward: the rest of the ride is either road or dirt track but there are one or two big climbs to bag and it's a manic macadam ribbon that staggers eastward into Glen Garry, kicking off with over 400ft (125m) of tarmac torture. Stick it in the granny and take sustenance from the grandiose scenery.

Take ten at Tomdoun then cross Loch Garry and climb into the forest, courtesy of Forest Enterprise. Mostly it's well-graded forest fire road that keeps to the contours before a final run down to the Garry river at Mandally. A short sojourn on the road round to Invergarry, then it's a killer, zigzag climb on the Great Glen Cycle Route into imposing pine plantations with the occasional panorama over the Great Glen. That's the day's climbing done, so you can enjoy the gentle, undulating run down through the forest to the A82 at Oich Bridge. Pick up the Caledonian Canal towpath to spin out those trail-worn legs along the GGCR to Fort Augustus. Tomorrow it's the Corrieyairack Pass so get a good night's rest! NOTE: If tomorrow's weather forecast is bad use the low-level route to avoid the Pass beginning in Mandally. Do not go on to Fort Augustus; overnight in Invergarry or Loch Lochy SYHA. This detour will add one day to your trip.

ARNISDALE Turn L (ESE, N then ESE) for 1m (1.6km) – passing through Glenfield – to footbridge over River Arnisdale then cross footbridge and turn L (ESE) for 1.7m (2.7km) – with sharp climb and crossing several fords – to another footbridge

DUBH over the Arnisdale near Dubh Lochain. Cross to
LOCHAIN N side of river.

Turn R (N then E) for 4m (6.4km) – passing N of lochans, SO (ESE) at T-junction by pylons at 2m (3.2km) and crossing Allt a' Choire Reidh burn

KINLOCH footbridge – to T-junction before ford in Kinloch
HOURN Hourn Forest. Turn R (S then SE) for 1m (1.6km) – over col – to path T-junction then keep R (S) for 0.5m/0.8km – dropping down to footbridge then joining track – to T-junction with C-road by

TOMDOUN Loch Hourn River. Turn L (ESE) for 15.5m (25km)

to Tomdoun Hotel (**accommodation available**).

Keep SO (E) for 2.5m (4km) to T-junction leading to bridge over Loch Garry then turn R (SSE) for 1.5m (2.4km) – crossing bridge and keeping SO at

GREENFIELD junctions – to Greenfield. Then swing R (S then E) for 5.5m (8.8km) – on obvious forest track keeping SO (E) at T-junctions at 1m (1.6km), 1.8m (2.9km), 2m (3.2km) and 2.5m (4km) then keeping L (SSE) at T-junction at 4.3m (7km) and R (E) at T-junction at 5m/8km - to T-junction at C-road. Keep SO (E) for 2m (3.2km) – passing T-junction with Great Glen Cycle Route (GGCR) to Laggan Bridge in Mandally at 1.3m (2.1km) – to T-junction with A82 at

INVERGARRY Invergarry (**accommodation available**). NOTE:

for 3m (4.8km) road route to Loch Lochy SYHA via Laggan Bridge turn R on A82.

LOW-LEVEL ROUTE AVOIDING CORRIEYAIRACK PASS (MANDALLY TO LAGGAN ON SPEY VIA GLEN SPEAN 55m (89km); NOT SHOWN ON MAPS.)

MANDALLY At Mandally turn R (ESE, S then SW) on GGCR track for 2m (3.2km) – up round Creag Liath spur

LAGGAN – to Laggan Bridge and A82. Keep R (SW)
BRIDGE alongside A82 to go on onto C-road for 2.5m

MAP 4

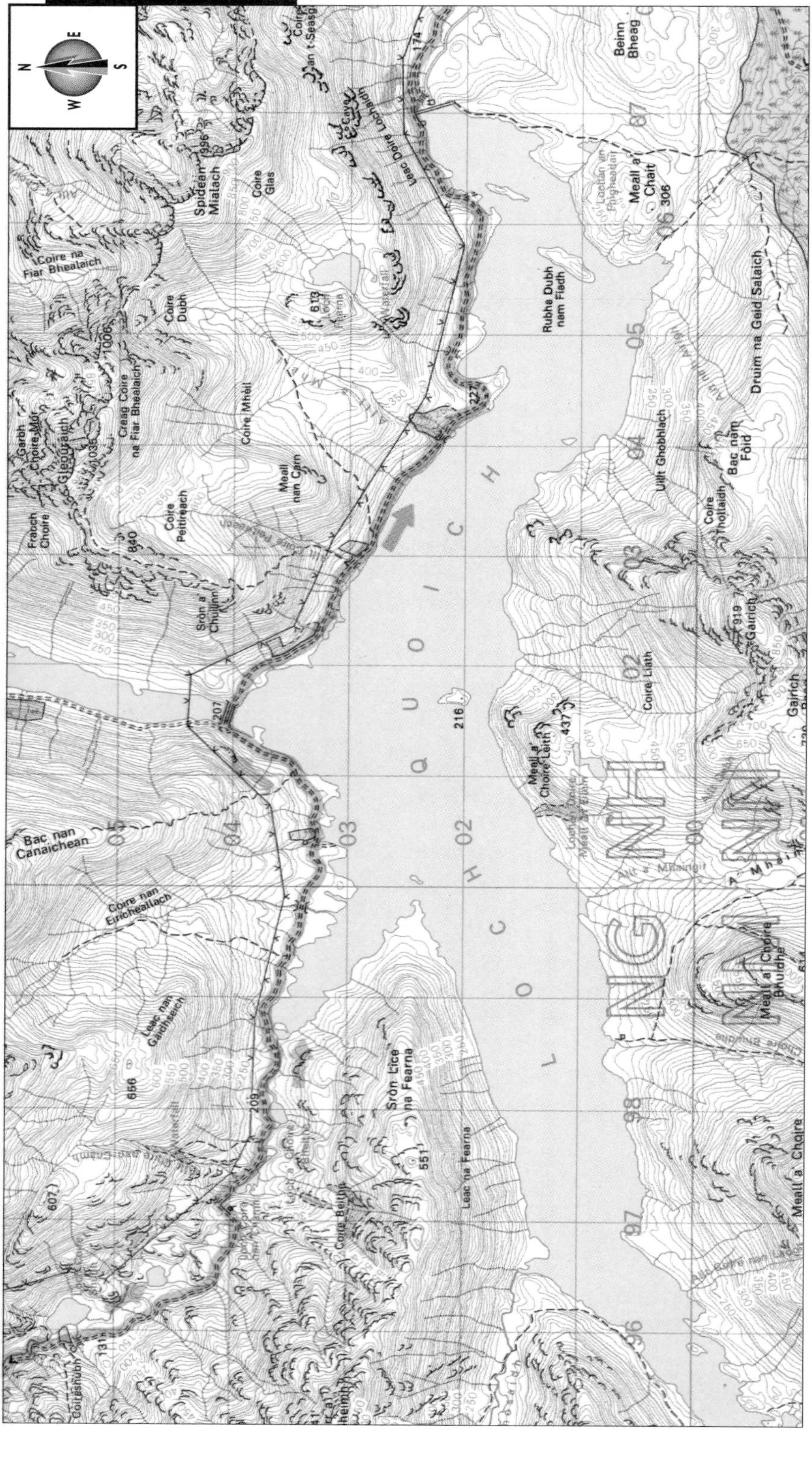
N
E
S
W
LOCH QUOICH
Spidean Mialach
Coire Glas
Coire na Fiar Bhealaich
Coire Dubh
Creag Coire na Fiar Bhealaich
Gleouraich
Garbh Choire Mór
Fraoch Choire
Coire Mheil
Meall nan Carn
Coire Peitireach
Sròn a' Chuilinn
Bac nan Canaichean
Coire nan Eiricheallach
Leac nan Gaidhseich
Sròn Lice na Fearna
Leac na Fearna
Coire Beithe
Beinn Bheag
Meall a Chait
Rubha Dubh nam Fiadh
Druim na Geid Salaich
Uilt Ghobhlach
Bac nam Foid
Coire Thollaidh
Gairich
Coire Liath
Meall a' Choire Léith
Meall a' Choire Bhuidhe
Meall a' Choire
NG
NM
174
207
209
216
227
306
437
551
613
656
840
919
996
1006
1035

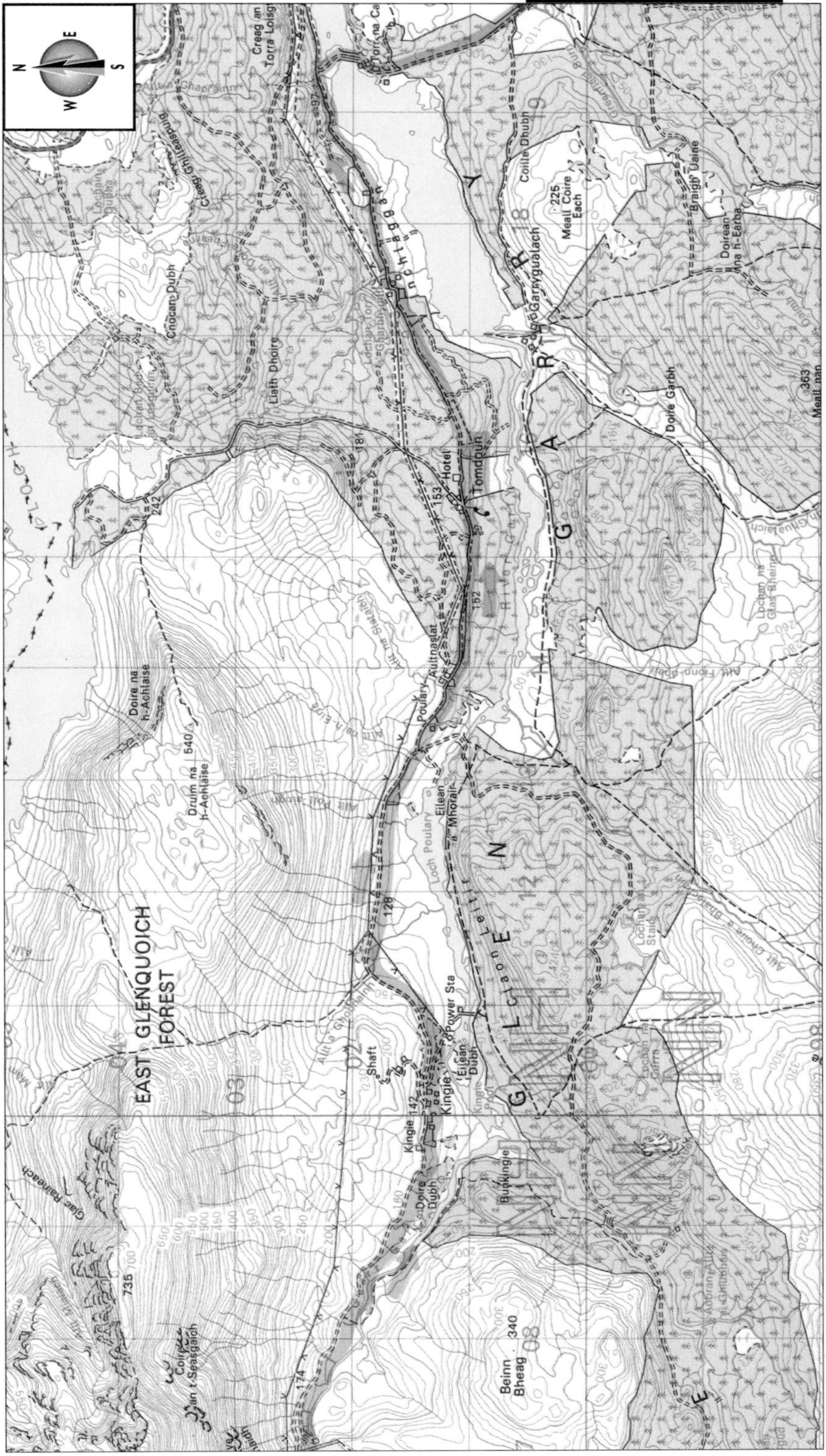
N
E
S
W
EAST GLENQUOICH FOREST
Doire na h-Achlaise
Druim na h-Achlaise
540
735
Glac Raineach
Coire an t-Seasgaich
Loch Poulary
Eilean a' Mhorair
Poulary
Aultnaslat
Tomdoun
Hotel
153
152
181
128
142
174
Kingie
Eilean Dubh
Power Sta
Shaft
Doire Dubh
Bunkingie
Beinn Bheag
340
Inchlaggan
Liath Dhoire
Cnocan Dubh
Creag an Torra Loisgte
Torr na Ca
Coille Dhubh
225
Meall Coire Each
Braigh Uaine
Doirean na h-Earba
Doire Garbh
363
Garrygualach
Lochan na Glas Bheinn
Lochan nan Stuc
242
197
G
L
E
N
G
A
R
R
Y
Claonelettir

(4km) to cross Kilfinnan bridge. Keep R (WSW then SW) for 0.75m (1.2km) – onto forest road – to T-junction then fork L (SSW) for 6m (9.6km) – on forest road by Loch Lochy – to B8005 at Clunes.

SPEAN BRIDGE

Turn L (SSW) for 3.6m (5.8km) to T-junction then fork L (SW) for 0.15m (0.25km) to next T-junction then turn L (SE) for 2.5m (4km) on B8004 – crossing Caledonian Canal – to T-junction with A82 by the Commando Memorial then turn R (SE) for 1.1m (1.8km) to Spean Bridge (cafés here) to T-junction just before 'Little Chef'.

Turn R (SSW) for 80yds (75m) to T-junction then fork L (SE) for 3m (4.8km) – joining track – to gated T-junction at Insh. Turn L (N) for 110yds (100m) to another gated T-junction then turn R (E) for 2m (3.2km) – on undulating, gated woodland track finally for open climb – to another gate. Go through and swing L (ENE) for 0.5m (0.8km) to gate by Monessie farm (please walk here). Go SO (N) for 0.25m (0.4km) – through gate – passing E of farm on track – to T-junction on bend then keep L (NNE) for 0.2m (0.3km) – on singletrack – to go over Monessie footbridge. Path turns R (SE) for 50yds (50m) then turn L (NE then ESE) for 0.2m (0.3km) – on track over railway – to T-junction then turn R (E then NNW) for 140yds (125m) to A86 at Achluachrach.

(**Accommodation available here**).
NOTE: For overnight at The Grey Corries Hostel by Roybridge Hotel, turn L (WNW) for 2m (3.2km).

ROYBRIDGE

Turn R (ESE) for 8.5m (13.6km) – past Glen Spean Resv – to track T-junction onto bridge then turn R (S) for 0.2m (0.3km) to T-junction by Luiblea then turn L (ENE then SSE) for 0.8m (1.2km) – over stile – up to T-junction. Turn R (S) for 1.3m (2.1km) to track T-junction with triangle island then fork L (E) for 0.8m (1.2km) to footbridge by southern-most Lochan na h-Earba.

Go SO (ESE) and almost immediately fork L (ESE) for 0.3m (0.5km) to T-junction then turn L (NE) for 2.5m (4km) – beside Lochan – to T-junction by northern Lochan na h-Earba. Keep R (NE) for 1.5m (2.4km) to T-junction after stile then keep R (NE) for 1m (1.6km) to track junction near Ardverikie House. Fork R (NNE) for 2.75m (4.4km) – keeping R (NE) onto drive – round Loch Laggan to A86 at Kinloch Laggan. Turn R (ENE) for 6.4m (10km), to Laggan (on Spey) (**accommodation available**).

LAGGAN

MAIN CTC ROUTE CONTINUES FROM MANDALLY:

INVERGARRY

Turn L (NW) for 0.25m (0.4km) to A87 in Invergarry then turn L (W) for 0.12m (0.2km) – past hotel and café to telephone box – to T-junction with GGCR then turn R (N) for 4m (6.4km) – up zigzags at first on forest track – to A82 at Oich Bridge. Go SO (E) for 120yds (115m) to the Caledonian Canal bridge then turn L (NNE) onto canal towpath for 4m (6.4km) to Fort Augustus (**accommodation available** – Abbey Backpackers recommended 2nd night).

CALEDONIAN CANAL

OFF-ROAD CODE
● **Guard against all risk of fire**
● **Fasten all gates**
● **Keep dogs under control**

A scenic ride along the Caledonian Canal.

MAP 6

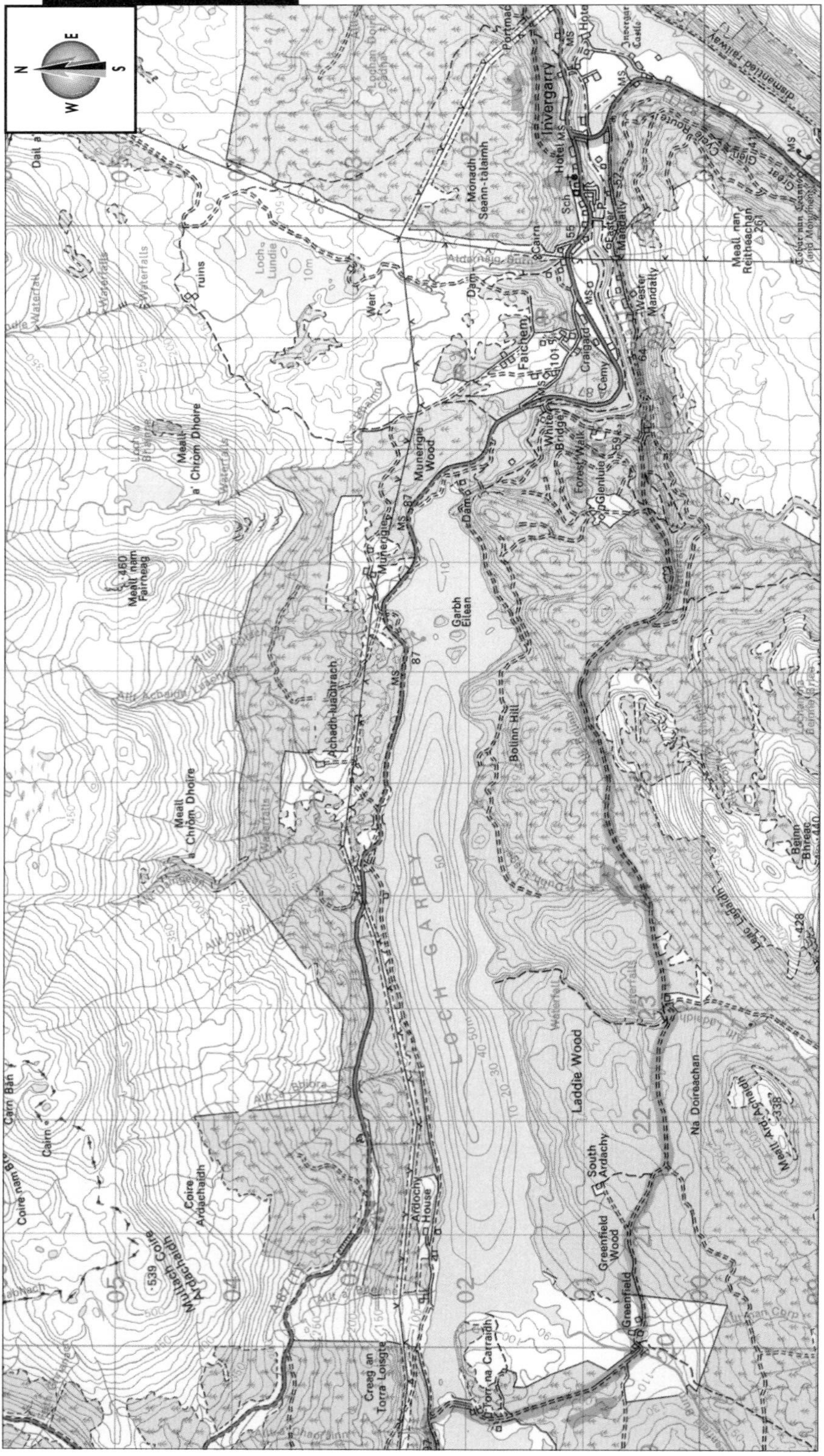

N
E
S
W
Invergarry
Hotel
Sch
Invergarry Castle
dismantled railway
Great Glen Cycle Route
Monadh Seann-talaimh
Easter Mandally
Wester Mandally
Meall nan Reitheachan
261
Loch Lundie
ruins
Waterfalls
Weir
Dam
Cairn
Faichem
Craigard
Cemy
White Bridge
Forest Walk
Glenluie
Meall a' Chrom Dhoire
Munerigie Wood
Munerigie
Garbh Eilean
Meall nam Pairneag
460
Achadh-luachrach
Bolinn Hill
LOCH GARRY
Allt Dubh
Laddie Wood
Waterfall
Na Doireachan
Meall Ard Achaidh
338
South Ardachy
Greenfield Wood
Greenfield
Ardachy House
Creag an Torra Loisgte
Torr na Carraidh
Coire Ardachaidh
Mullach Coire Ardachaidh
539
Carn Ban
Cairn
Beinn Bhreac
440
428

MAP 7

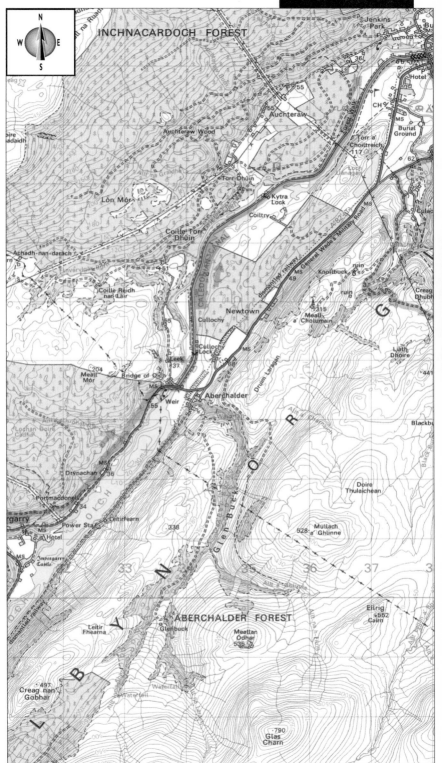

INCHNACARDOCH FOREST

Jenkins Park

Auchteraw

Auchteraw Wood

Torr a' Choitreich
117

Burial Ground

Torr Dhùin

Kytra Lock

Coiltry

Lòn Mòr

Coille Torr Dhùin

Achadh-nan-darach

Inverroy

Coille Rèidh nan Làir

Knoltbuck

ruin

Creag Dhubh

Newtown

Meall a' Cholumain
315

Cullochy

Liath Dhoire

Cullochy Lock

Meall Mòr
204

Leek

Bridge of Oich

Aberchalder

Drum Laragan

Weir

Blackbu

Drynachan
36

Doire Thulaichean

Portmacdonell

Mullach a' Ghlinne
528

Invergarry

Power Sta

Ceitlefearn

Invergarry Castle

338

33   35   36   37

ABERCHALDER FOREST

Eirig Cairn
552

Leitir Fhearna

Glenbuck

Meallan Odhar
535

Creag nan Gobhar
497

Waterfall

Glas Charn
790

DAY 3 Maps 8 – 12

FORT AUGUSTUS TO GLEN FESHIE
45m (72km), 21m (34km) off-road; 4250ft/1285m climbing.
Summits and passes: **Corrieyairack Pass 2550ft (772m); Inshriach Forest 1200ft (360m).**

It's not often that the authorities see fit to warn travellers that the road ahead is dangerous but **General Wade's** winding track over the **Corrieyairack Pass** is an exception. Take heed and if the weather's bad take the low level route via **Glen Spean.**

But if Nature sees fit to unplug a fine day then you're in for some terminal pass storming. Today's height gain is packed into one severe, leg-straining ascent – 3000ft (910m) of it – that's a killer even when riding light! Backpackers be prepared to walk the last mile or two but before that, Wade's road slots in some spicy technical sections and even the occasional descent. A handy pointer to what's in store is to keep an eye on those marching pylons.

Over the top for the famous **Corrieyairack** zigzags. It's a slalom over shattered rock. A mind-bending technical run that demands a steady hand on the anchors and a quick wit to pick the right lines. Take ten after the last bend to steady the nerves and give those aching arms and legs time to recover – there's plenty more fun to come! From here to **Melgarve** the old military road is an amazing ride. Fast and loose, it dips and dives down the valley with tricky bits here and there that steadily build into boulder field. We felt in manic mood and rode the lot but the ping-pong routine might seem pointless when there's ample room to pootle alongside.

It all goes quiet after **Melgarve,** turns to tarmac and your next off-road excursion comes after you've passed **Ruthven Barracks** (well worth a walk round if you've got time). Don't tear off up **Glen Tromie:** the C-t-C takes a hairpin left up to **Drumguish** before heading off into **Inshriach Forest.** There's a short 'n' sweet sweep down to the fords at **Balleguish** where there's little alternative to getting wet feet (one of the footbridges had disintegrated!). Vague grass track finally asserts itself, climbs up into pine plantation on forest-fire road before dropping down to meet tarmac in **Glen Feshie.** A quick run up-river, swap sides, then downstream on green singletrack interrupted by stream crossings. Be sure to pick up a series of marker posts that treat you to a short spell of sinuous singletrack round **Achlean** farm to tarmac road head. It's downhill – as near as dammit – all the way to Glen Feshie's **Balachroick** hostel.

FORT AUGUSTUS

At Fort Augustus turn R (S) on A82 for 0.1m (0.15km) to T-junction with B862 then keep L (S, towards Whitebridge) for 0.7m (1.15km) to T-junction with C-road then turn R (SW) for 1.25m (2km) to X-roads with Corrieyairack road track (GR373072, 0.5m/0.8km SW of Ardachy Lodge).

ARDACHY LODGE

Turn L through gate (SE) for 5.3m (8.5km) – on obvious roller-coaster track, keeping SO at T-junction at 1.1m (1.8km) and ignoring track that cuts through first zigzag climb – to bridge. Take a rest, the real climb is from here. Keep SO (SSW then E) for 2.1m (3.4km) climb – with pylons shadowing the route – to Corrieyairack Pass (2550ft/772m and the highest point on the Coast-to-Coast).

CORRIEY-AIRACK PASS

Keep SO (E then ESE) for 7.5m (12km) – down through 6 zigzags (a bit loose, so take care) then on less steep track which turns into a boulder field for a while – to Garva Bridge then go SO (ESE) on C-road for 7m (11.2km) to T-junction with A86 in Laggan (on Spey) (**accommodation available**).

GARVA BRIDGE

BIKE CARE

After riding

● **Treat your bike kindly and it'll be a reliable friend. At the end of a day, hammering and being hammered by Highland trails, the last thing you want to do is bike maintenance but at the very least you should clean (a quick spray with a hose should suffice), lube (a dose of water-dispersant followed by oil on the chain) then check it over. Check right after a ride and you'll remember all those little mechanicals that have been niggling you during the day plus wet mud washes off easily, dried mud is a lot harder to shift. Set it up for the following day and you'll sleep easy, get up late and still be able to mount up and ride out. A daily check-up should include brake blocks, tyres, wheels, gears and fixings for pannier racks. It's a good idea to keep an eye on the chain, headset, stem, cranks and seat post.**

MAP 8

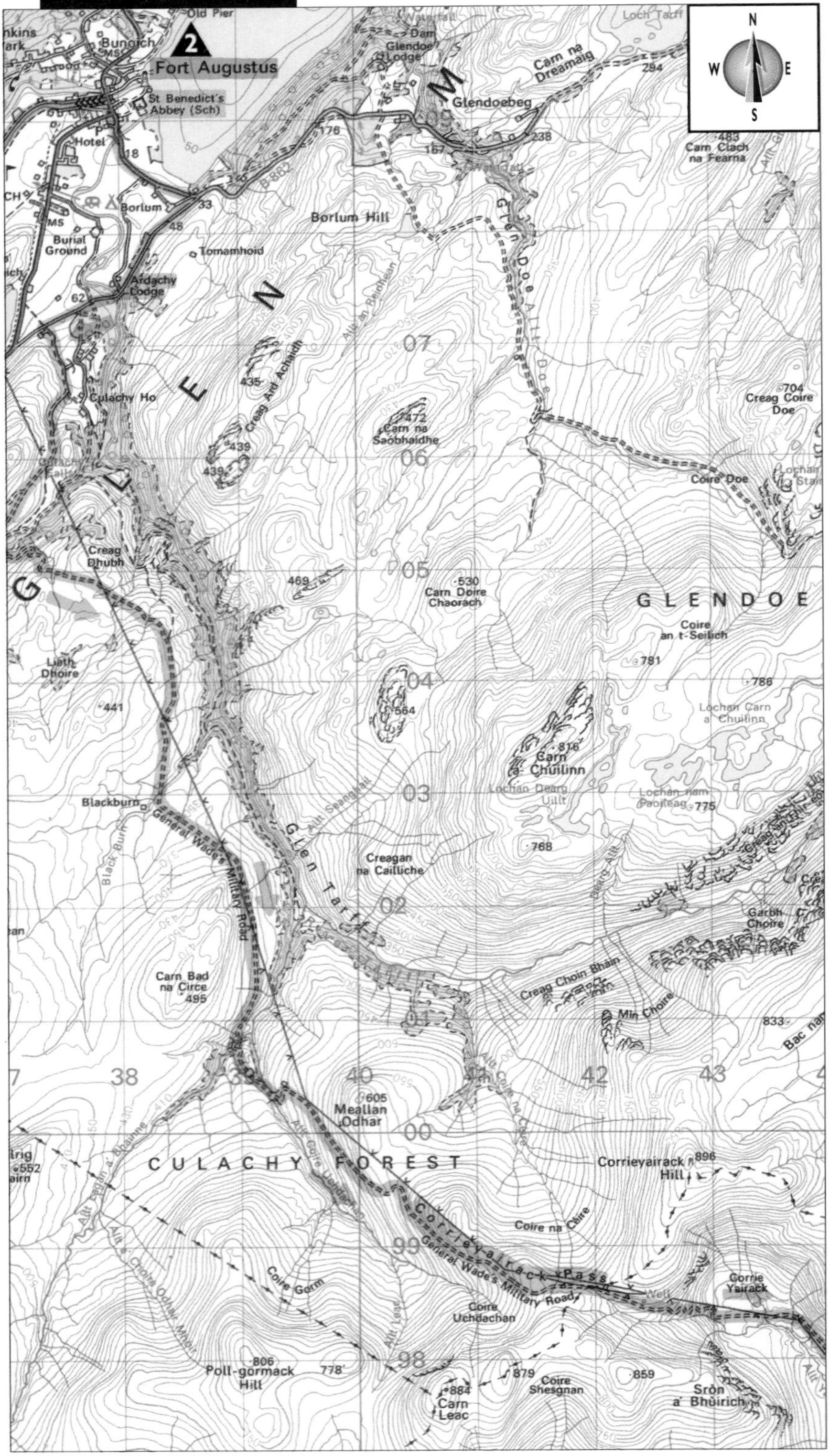

N
W
E
S
Old Pier
Bunoich
2
Fort Augustus
St Benedict's Abbey (Sch)
Hotel
Borlum
Burial Ground
Tomamhoid
Ardachy Lodge
Culachy Ho
Waterfall
Dam
Glendoe Lodge
Glendoebeg
Carn na Dreamaig
Loch Taff
Carn Clach na Fearna
B 862
Borlum Hill
Glen Doe
Allt Doe
Creag Ard Achaidh
Carn na Saobhaidhe
Creag Coire Doe
Coire Doe
Creag Dhubh
Carn Doire Chaorach
GLENDOE
Coire an t-Seilich
Liath Dhoire
Lochan Carn a' Chuilinn
Carn a' Chuilinn
Lochan Dearg Uillt
Lochan nam Faoileag
Blackburn
Black Burn
General Wade's Military Road
Glen Tarff
Allt Seangaich
Creagan na Cailliche
Garbh Choire
Carn Bad na Circe
Creag Choin Bhain
Min Choire
Meallan Odhar
CULACHY FOREST
Corrieyairack Hill
Coire na Ciste
Corrieyairack Pass
Coire Gorm
Coire Uchdachan
Allt Coire Uchdachan
Corrie Yairack
Well
Poll-gormack Hill
Carn Leac
Coire Shesgnan
Sròn a' Bhùirich
Allt Coire na Ciste
G
L
E
N
M
07
06
05
04
03
02
01
00
99
98
38
39
40
42
43

MAP 9

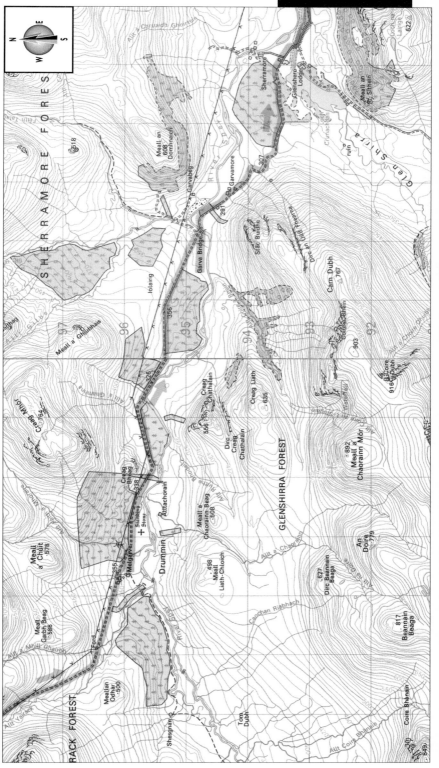

**NEWTON-
MORE**

KINGUSSIE

**TROMIE
BRIDGE**

Continue SO (E) on A86 for 5m (8km) – through Newtonmore (**pubs, shops and accommodation available here**) – to T-junction with B970 in Kingussie (**pubs, shops and accommodation available here**). Turn R (SSE) for 1.5m (2.4km) – past BR station and Ruthven Barracks – to T-junction with track just after Tromie Bridge.

 WET WEATHER ROUTE FROM TROMIE BRIDGE AVOIDING BAILEGUISH FORD: Keep on B970 (N) for 3m (4.8km) to T-junction with C-road just after Feshiebridge then turn R (SSE) for 0.5m (0.8km) to RH bend in Lagganlia. NOTE: for recommended 3rd night in Balachroick Hostel keep on C-road S for a further 1m (1.6km).

 BIKE CARE

Taccoed wheel

● **Remove the tyre then use brute force to push the offending bows back in line. Rest two apexes on opposite sides of the rim on two logs or rocks, the bow curving away from the contact point. Grab opposite sides of the rim and shove down. Only one log or rock handy? Then wedge a bowed-out section of the wheel against it – or a tree – at an angle, rest the opposite sector on your knees or body and shove. No handy tree or boulder, then whack the apex of a bow hard on the ground. Re-fit the wheel, fine adjust with a spoke key then re-fit the tyre. If you still have to release the brake in order to ride then it's probably better to leg it.**

MAP 12

MAIN CTC ROUTE CONTINUES FROM
TROMIE BRIDGE:

Turn R (S) for 0.12m (0.2km) to T-junction then
take hairpin turn L (NE) for 0.25m (0.4km) to X-
roads in Drumguish. Turn R (SE) for 2.1m (3.4km)

DRUMGUISH

– into forest and SO (ESE) at junctions, finally
down zigzags – to gate. Go SO (E) for 0.1m
(0.15km) to fork R (SSE) for 0.5m (0.8km) –
fording Allt Chomhraig and swinging L (SE then

BAILEGUISH

NE) round Baileguish – to cross footbridge. Fork
L (NE) for 0.1m (0.15km) – on undefined path –

CORARN-
STILMORE

to green track then turn R (ESE) for 0.25m
(0.4km) up to gate by Corarnstilmore.

Go SO (ESE) for 1.2m (1.9km) – on track up into
forest and keeping SO (SE) at junctions – to
tarmac unclassified county road. Turn R (SSE,
signed Blair Atholl) for 0.5m (0.8km) to track T-
junction then fork L (ESE) for 80yds (75m) – over
River Feshie – to field. Turn L (N) for 1m (1.6km)
– on vague singletrack alongside River Feshie,
through gate, then follow diversion posts around
Achlean farm – to C-road end. Follow C-road (N)
for 4.4m (7km) –
NOTE: **accommodation available** at

BALACHROIK

Balachroick Hostel, recommended 3rd night, 2m
(3.2km) down this road – to T-junction with
singletrack on LH bend at Lagganlia.

 OFF-ROAD CODE
- **Keep to Public Rights of Way
  across farmland**
- **Use gates and stiles to cross
  boundaries**
- **Leave livestock, crops and
  machinery alone**
- **Take your litter home**
- **Do not contaminate water**
- **Protect wild flora and fauna**

MAP 10

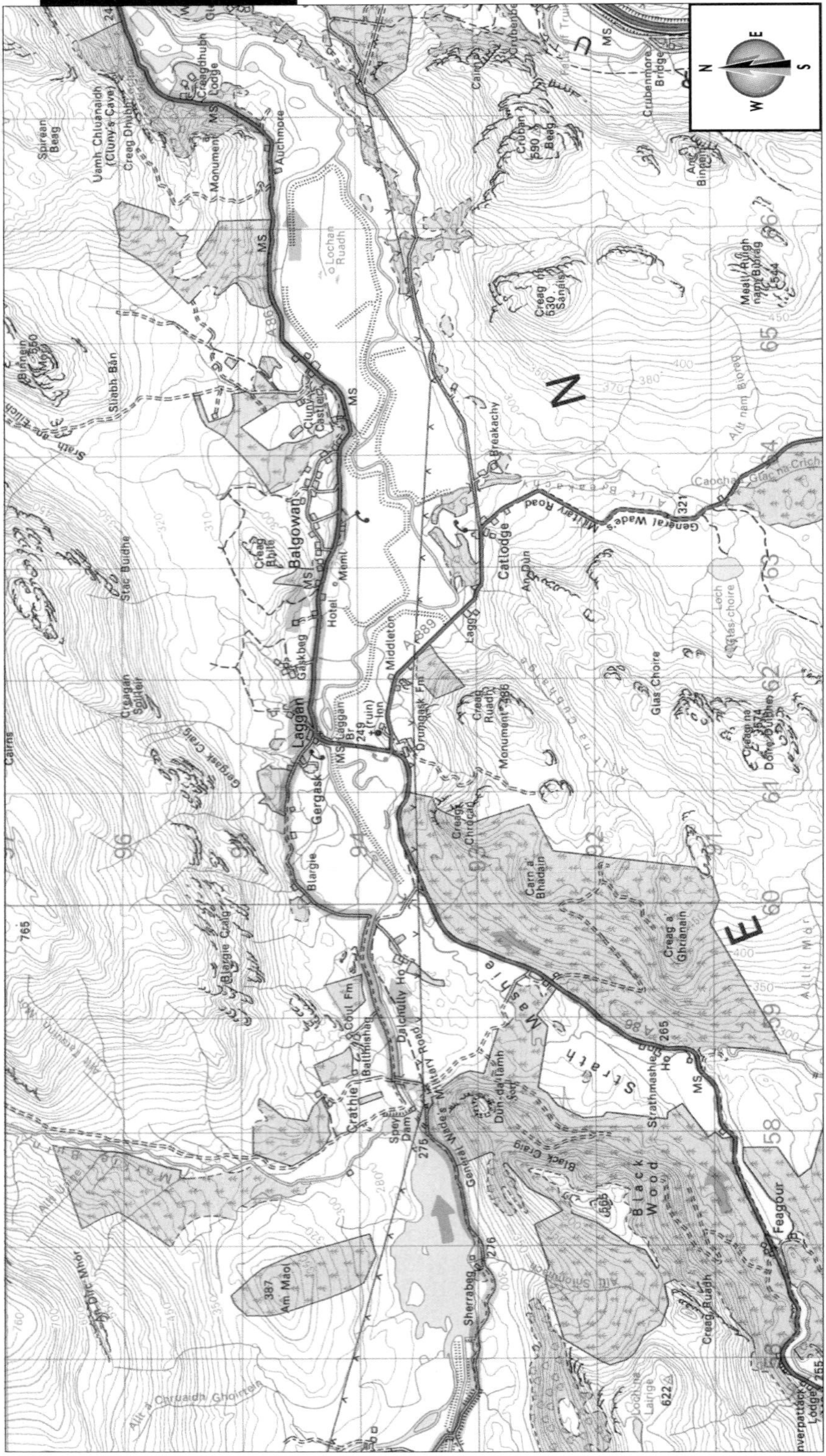

Laggan
Balgowan
Gergask
Blargie
Cluny Castle
Catlodge
Breakachy
Middleton
Drumgask Fm
Crathie
Coul Fm
Dalchully Ho
Spey Dam
Sherrabeg
Strathmashie Ho
Feagour
Black Wood
Creag Ruadh
Auchmore
Crubenmore Bridge
General Wade's Military Road
Strath Mashie
A86
A889
Am Maol
Lochan Ruadh
Carn a' Bhadain
Creag a' Ghrianain
Glas Choire
Stac Buidhe
Sliabh Bàn
Binnein

MAP 11

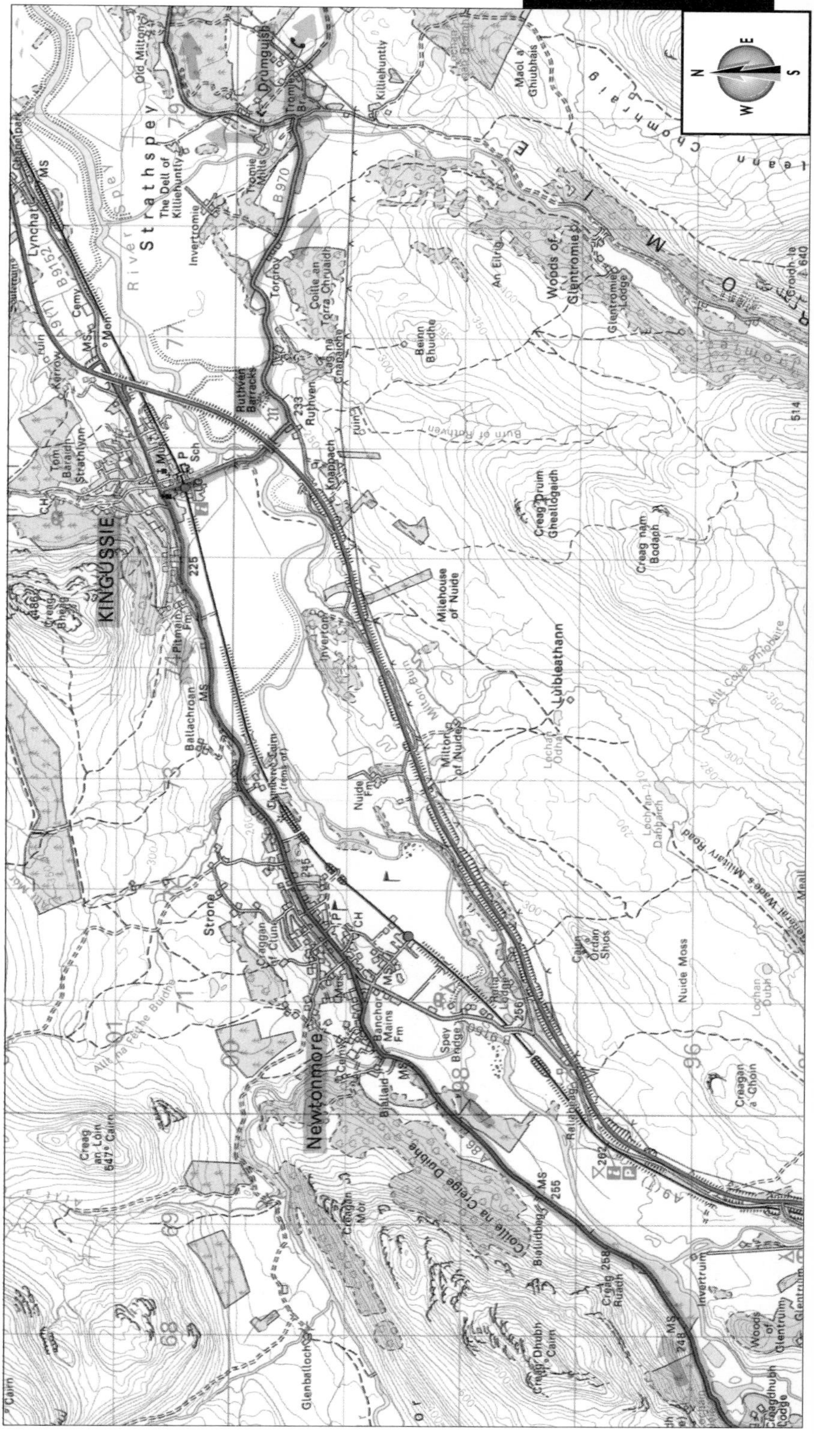

DAY 4 Maps 13 – 16

GLEN FESHIE TO TOMINTOUL
34m (55km), 26m (42km) off-road; 2560ft/775m climbing.

Summits and passes: Ryvoan Bothy 1350ft (405m); Carn a' Chnuic 1350ft (405m); Eag Mhór Pass 1410ft (427m); Tom an t-suidhe Mhóir 1560ft (472m); Stronachavie 1300ft (395m); Tomintoul 1140ft (345m).

Okay so there's no mega-climbs like the **Corrieyairack** but make no mistake this is a tough day – most of it's off-road. First up is forest fire road with handy blue-topped posts – marking a cross-country ski-run – to keep you on track; relax and spin. Back to track at **Loch an Eilein** but here you're in **Nature Reserve** and hikers abound so keep a weather eye out for walkers. The off-roading's fun – not tricky but with sufficient twists and turns to add the essential interest, especially if it's wet.

Cross the **Cairngorm Club Footbridge**, trip down a rag-tag rooty run then before long the trail gets rubbly where it's washed out. But it's a short stretch and soon you're spinning through the forest, over a stile then down fast forest fire road. Not too quick or you'll overshoot your turning and end up on the main road round **Loch Morlich**. The sandy track round the south side's much more fun.

Loch Morlich is an ideal lunch stop before heading up **Glen More** and onto the heather-clad heathland of the **Abernethy Forest**. We were there in May riding through sombre braes of burnt umber, but in late summer this must be a sea of shimmering purple. Mind you, we did have snow-capped **Cairngorm** mountains as a back drop and the track riding is superb. None of the finely graded forest fire road, just rough stuff and hard-pack – when dry. Let the rubber hum and slipstream roar all the way down to **Forest Lodge**.

Forest Lodge is a busy spot in summer so cycle with care. You're soon back to sandy track, slipped in between majestic pine trees. In fine weather sunlight flickers, the scent lingers and the beauty of these woodlands will invite you to saunter. The track tumbles off the shoulder of **Carn a' Chnuic** down to **Faesheallach Burn** for a boot-wetting ford crossing. singletrack winds its way up the valley ahead, onto the open moor where it takes to a small ridge on vague Landrover track. Fine views stretch way over **Strathspey**.

Into the trees and the C-t-C all but disappears. Don't panic, just swing right, drop down to the fence and follow the path up the amazing ravine of **Eag Mhór**. It's tricky to ride – there's a couple of wheel-grabbing gullies – until you quit the forest then dial in the

MAP 13

trial skills for a roller-coaster route across the scree slopes. A final fast blast down shooting track finales with a drop-off into the ford over Dorback Burn. Most of the C-t-C crew rode right across and it's not narrow!

A quick foray across fields, slip in some tarmac to Dorback Lodge then it's the final off-road treat before Tomintoul. From here on prime-time descents top the bill on the C-t-C. Of course that means climbing too but be positive – what goes up must come down! Down to Burn of Brown is a divine, crooked cart track with rut and rubble to up the adrenaline factor and a ford to finish it off. A twisty pathway follows the burn bank before tackling the contours head-on up by the pine plantation. The efforts on this last off-road climb are rewarded by a fine forest fire road descent to the Bridge of Avon. Tarmac to Tomintoul to tone down on with fine views up the Avon valley. That's where you're heading tomorrow.

GLEN FESHIE	Go SO (N) for 1.1m (1.8km) – keeping SO at track junctions – to five-way X-roads. Fork R (E then ENE then N) for 1.6m (2.6km) – following
INSHRIACH	blue-topped guide posts – to B970 at Inshriach.
	Turn R (ENE) for 2.2m (3.5km) to T-junction at monument then turn R (SE) for 0.75m (1.2km) to T-junction with island then keep SO (SSE) for 0.8m (1.2km) – almost immediately to fork L
LOCH AN EILEIN	keeping Loch an Eilein to your R – to track T-junction just beyond footbridge then turn L (ESE) for 0.7m (1.15km) to track T-junction and fork L (NE, signed 'Cyclists') for 50yds (50m) to next T-junction. Fork L (E) for 110yds (100m) to X-roads
CAIRNGORM CLUB FOOT-BRIDGE	at forest edge. Go SO (E, signed 'Lairig Ghru') for 0.75m (1.2km) to zigzag L/R (Effectively SO) (ESE) over Cairngorm Club footbridge.
ALLT DRUIDH	Continue (ESE) for 1m (1.6km) – on singletrack alongside Allt Druidh then at 0.7m (1.15km) swing L (ENE) away from stream – to singletrack X-roads then go SO (NE) for 1m (1.6km) – over stile – to T-junction with track. Fork L (N) for

MAP 12

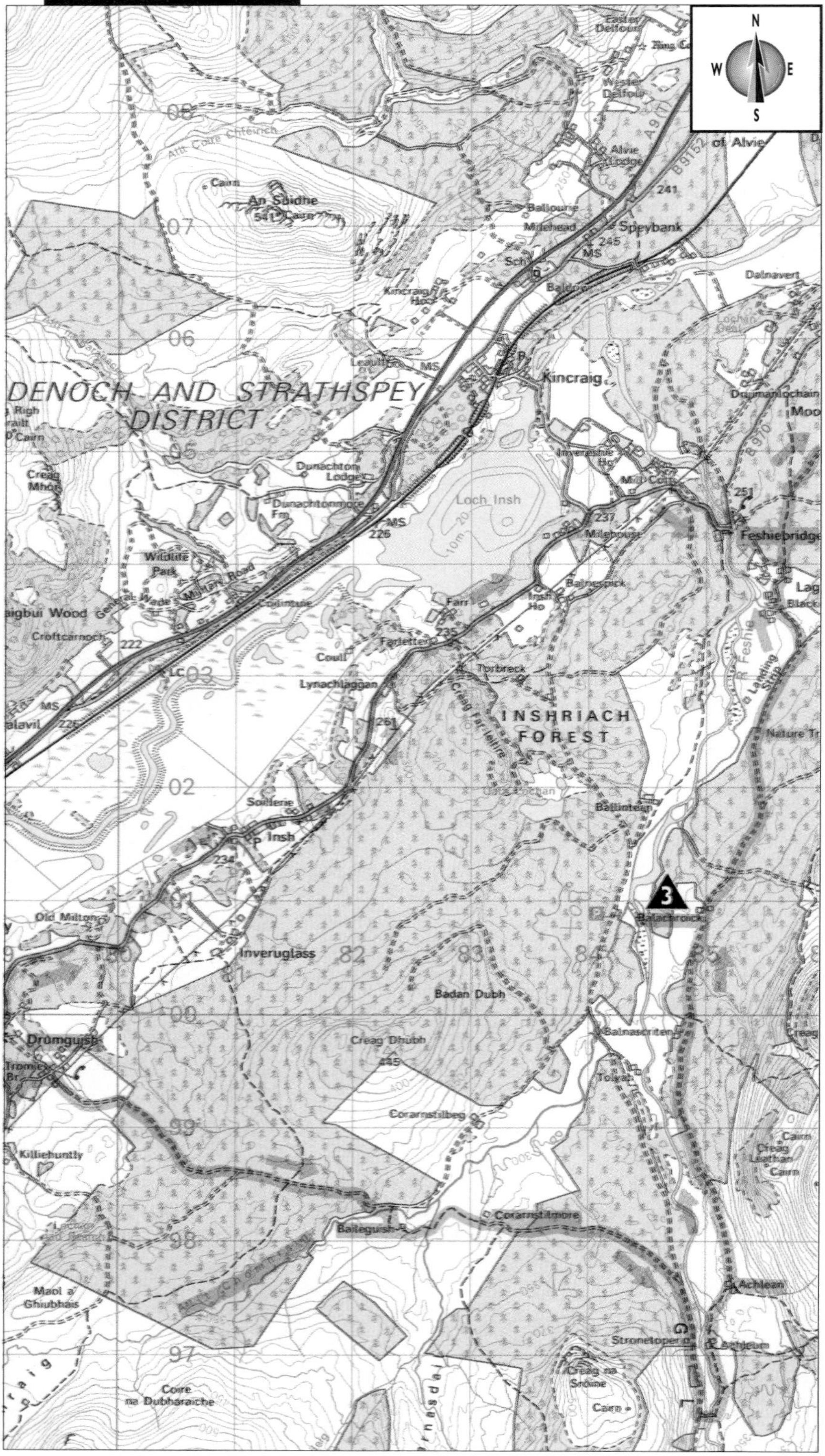

N
S
W
E
Easter Delfour
Wester Delfour
Alvie Lodge
of Alvie
An Suidhe
Cairn
Balloune
Milehead
Speybank
Sch
Baldow
Kincraig Ho
Dalnavert
Leault
Kincraig
Loch Insh
BADENOCH AND STRATHSPEY DISTRICT
Creag Mhor
Dunachton Lodge
Dunachtonmore Fm
Inveresshie Ho
Mill Cott
Milehouse
Feshiebridge
Wildlife Park
General Wade's Military Road
Balnespick
Insh Ho
Farr
Farletter
Croftcarnoch
Coull
Torbreck
Lynachlaggan
INSHRIACH FOREST
Nature Trail
Soillerie
Insh
Ballintean
Old Milton
Balachroick
Inveruglass
Badan Dubh
Drumguish
Balnascriten
Creag Dhubh
Tolvah
Corarnstilbeg
Killiehuntly
Creag Leathan
Baileguish
Corarnstilmore
Maol a' Ghiubhais
Achlean
Stronetoper
Coire na Dubharaiche
Creag na Sroine
Cairn
3

MAP 13

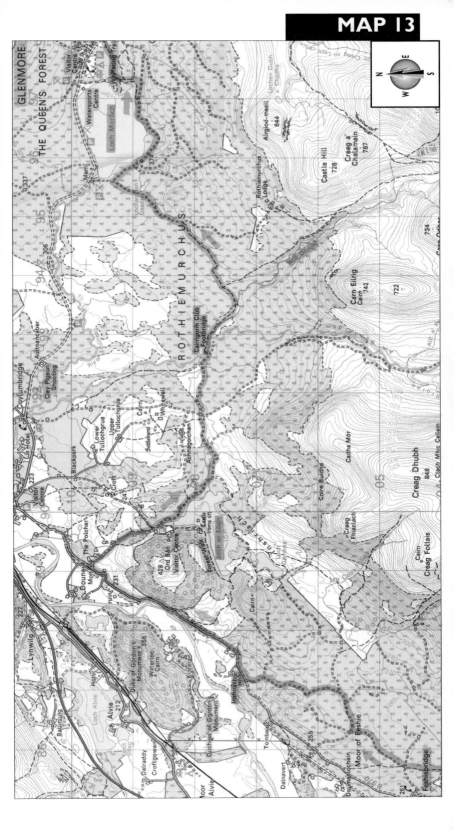

LOCH MORLICH

0.9m (1.3km) to track T-junction (easy to over-shoot) by Loch Morlich. Turn R (SE) for 0.4m (0.6km) – over stile – to T-junction then fork L (SE) for 1.1m (1.8km) – along S shore of Loch Morlich – to T-junction then turn L (NNE) for 0.3m (0.5km) – over footbridge – to T-junction.

GLENMORE FOREST PARK VISITOR CENTRE

Turn R (ESE) for 0.25m (0.4km) – by river – to T-junction then fork L (NNE) for 0.2m (0.3km) – away from river – to X-roads with C-road in Glen More Forest Park Visitor Centre (turn L for 0.3m/0.5km to café and SYHA).

GLENMORE LODGE

RYVOAN BOTHY

FOREST LODGE

Go SO (E, towards Glenmore Lodge) for 2.2m (3.5km) – picking up track beyond Glenmore Lodge – to T-junction then keep L (NE) for 2.6m (4.2km) – passing Ryvoan Bothy, into Abernethy Forest keeping L at T-junction at 1.6m (2.6km) and SO at 2.4m (3.8km) at T-junction off L to Rynettin – to track T-junction then fork L (ENE) for 1.2m (1.9km) to X-roads. Fork R (NE) for 0.1m (0.15km) to X-roads at Forest Lodge car-park.

LOCH A' CHNUIC

Go SO (NE) for 0.6m (1km) – keeping L at T-junction soon after then down over bridge – to staggered X-roads. Turn R (SSW) for 3.1m (5km) – keeping L at junction at 1.1m (1.8km), over ford, SO at X-roads at 1.5m (2.4km), SO at T-junction at 1.7m (2.7km), swinging R at T-junction at 2.8m (4.5km) and passing Loch a' Chnuic – to T-junction (on RH bend and not obvious) above Faesheallach Burn.

EAG MHÓR

Go SO (E) for 0.5m (0.8km) – over river and up side of valley on singletrack – to vague T-junction then keep R (NE) for 0.3m (0.5km) – up ridge on vague Landrover track into trees where it peters out. Swing R (E) for 110yds (100m) down to fence then turn L (NE) for 0.12m (0.2km) – alongside fence – to gate in Eag Mhór ravine.

Keep SO (ENE then N) for 1.2m (1.9km) – on singletrack then on shooting track – to Dorback Burn ford then go SO (N then WNW) for 0.3m (0.5km) – onto pasture land – to track T-junction

DORBACK LODGE

then turn R (N) for 0.5m (0.8km) to C-road at Ballintuim. Turn R (SSE) for 1m (1.6km) to track T-junction past Dorback Lodge then turn R (ENE) for 0.15m (0.25km) up to gate.

LETTER- AITTEN

STRON- ACHAVIE

TOMINTOUL

Go SO (E) for 0.75m (1.2km) to T-junction then turn R (SE then NE) for 2m (3.2km) – past Letteraitten and keeping R at T-junction at 0.9m (1.3km) then down winding track – to Burn of Brown ford. Cross river then turn L (NE) for 0.5m (0.8km) – downstream – to end of plantation then turn R (E) 50yds (50m) – up vague singletrack beside trees – to T-junction with track. Turn R (SE then NE) for 0.8m (1.2km) to gated T-junction at Stronachavie then turn R (E) for 1.5m (2.4km) – down through plantation – to T-junction with A939 at Bridge of Avon. Turn R (ESE) for 2.2m (3.5km) to Tomintoul centre. (**accommodation available – recommended 4th night**).

A watery ride into the ford over Dorback Burn.

MAP 14

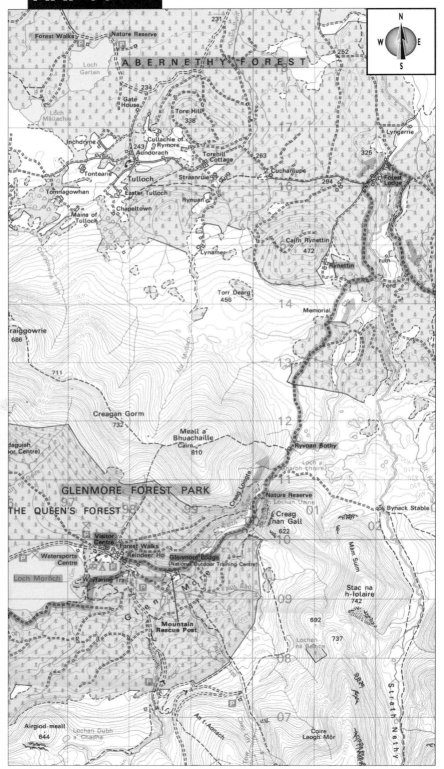

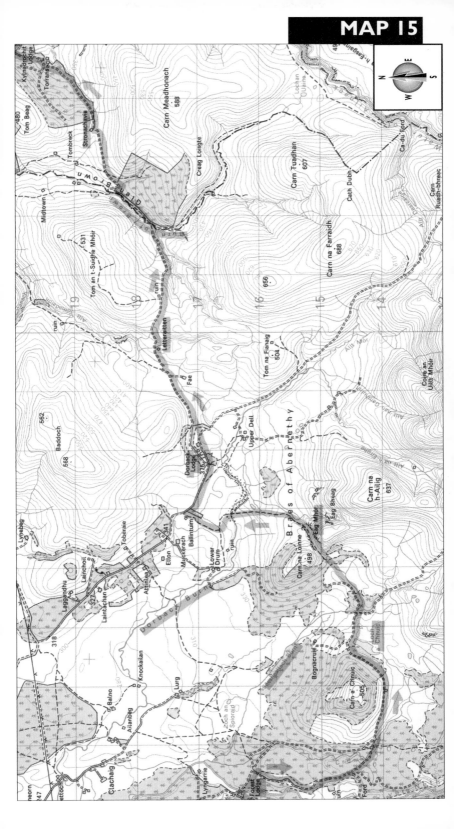

MAP 15

DAY 5 Maps 16 – 19

TOMINTOUL TO BALLATER

34m (55km), 21m (33km) off-road; 2050ft (625m) climbing.
Summits and passes: Culardoch 2400ft (730m); Felagie 1140ft (345m).

Described by John Fulton as his favourite day on the C-t-C, this leg scores high on the scenic factor and slots in a short section of fun-time footpath: a leg-busting climb with a totally brilliant downhill all the way to Braemar as a just reward for all that height-gain pain.

First of all be sure to get a weather report and skip Culardoch if it looks bad, plus there's one or two fords so keep a check on heaven-sent water. Riding through Glen Avon is easy cart track cruising, right into the Cairngorm mountains, so apart from the scenery that surrounds you, the fun doesn't start 'til the Avon hangs a right. Glen Builg lies straight ahead for some height-gain and a spell on my favourite sort of singletrack that dips and dives, twists and weaves along the bouldery, heather-clad braes by Loch Builg.

Too short; back to track for the lung-busting climb over the shoulders of Culardoch – mountain vistas abound – to get dialled straight into an awesome descent that starts a touch rocky but soon settles into prime-time slipstream roar and rut-hopping. A curtain of quiet descends as tyres are hushed on the pine-needle carpet that covers the tracks in the Braemar forests and all too soon that long, long downhill is done and you're climbing up the lane past Felagie for the tarmac tone-down to Ballater.

TOMINTOUL	At T-junction in Tomintoul where A939 turns sharp L (ENE) go SO (SE) for 0.2m (0.3km) to X-roads then turn R (SW) for 0.7m (1.15km) to T-junction with track then fork L (S) for 8.8m
INCHRORY	(14km) – up E side of Glen Avon, passing Inchrory lodge, keeping SO at T-junction by bridge at 7.8m
GLEN BUILG	(12.5km) then up E side of Glen Builg – to ford. Zigzag R/L (effectively SO) (SSE) over Builg Burn for 0.5m (0.8km) – keeping R at T-junction at 0.12m (0.2km) – to cross another ford. Keep SO (SSE) for 1.1m (1.8km) – on track then singletrack
LOCH BUILG	along E side of Loch Builg swinging R between Loch Builg and the small Lochan Oir after fence

line at 1m (1.6km) – to track T-junction then turn L (ESE) for 0.3m (0.5km) to T-junction.

WET WEATHER ROUTE TO BALLATER AVOIDING CULARDOCH (MOST OF ROUTE NOT SHOWN ON MAPS HERE):
Go SO (ESE) for 4.2m (6.8km) – crossing River Gairn – to T-junction just after Daldownie then keep L (ENE) for 3m (5km) – down the Gairn valley – to the B976 at Braenaloin. Turn L (NE) for 1m (1.6km) to T-junction with A939 at Gairnshiel Lodge then turn R (ENE, towards Ballater) for 5m (8km) to T-junction with A93 then turn L (E) for 2m (3.2km) – through Ballater (recommended 5th night accommodation) – to Station Square.

BALLATER

MAIN CTC ROUTE CONTINUES FROM LOCHAN OIR:
Turn R (S) for 0.4m (0.6km) to T-junction just after crossing bridge then turn R (SSE) for 1m (1.6km) – on obvious track up Gairn valley – to swing L (S) for 3.3m (5.3km) – over shoulder of Culardoch (track swings R here) and keeping SO at T-junction soon after then long descent – to bridge over Allt Cúl.

CULARDOCH

ALLT CÚL

OFF-ROAD CODE
- ● Take special care on country roads
- ● Make no unnecessary noise
- ● Cycle only on permitted Rights of Way
- ● Give way to horse riders and walkers
- ● Do not ride in such a manner that you are a danger to others

MAP 16

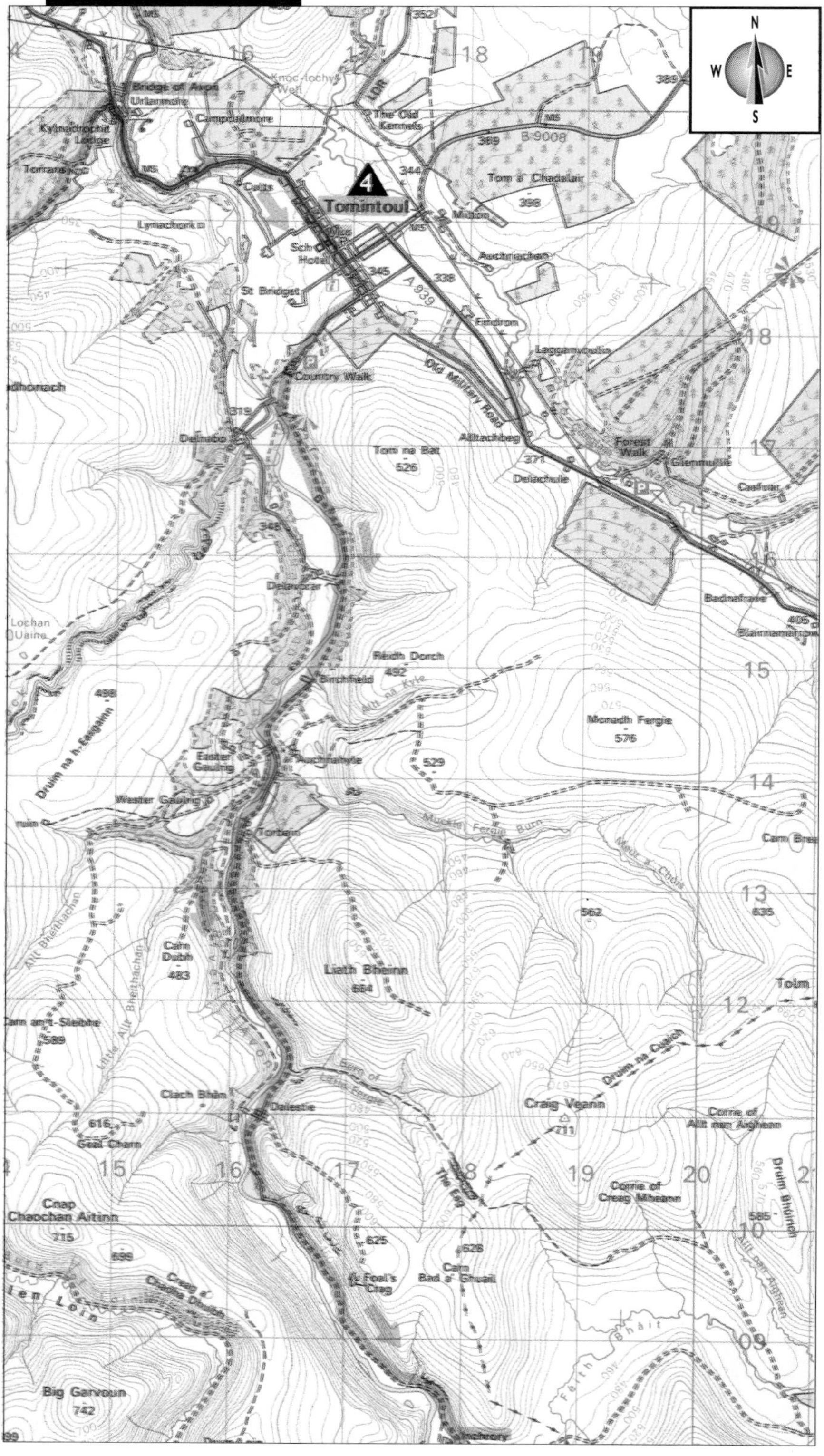

N W E S

Bridge of Avon
Urlanmore
Kylnadrochid Lodge
Tomanabrach
Knockrochy
Wall
The Old Kennels
Campdalemore
B-9008
Tom a' Chadalair
398
Cults
Tomintoul
Milton
Auchriachan
Sch
Hotel
St Bridget
345
338
A 939
Findron
Laggantoulin
Delnabo
315
Country Walk
Old Military Road
Alltachbeg
Delachuile
Forest Walk
Glenmullie
Castron
Tom na Bat
526
371
348
Delavorar
Badnafrave
405
Blairnamarrow
Lochan
Uaine
Réidh Dorch
492
Birchfield
Allt na Kyle
Monadh Fergie
576
498
Drum na h-Seilbhinn
Easter Gauling
Wester Gauling
Auchnahyle
529
Muckle Fergie Burn
Meur a' Choin
Carn Brea
Torbain
muim
562
13
635
Cairn Dubh
483
Liath Bheinn
664
Alt Bhebhachan
Tolm
12
Carn amt-Sleibhe
589
Little Allt Bhebhachan
Clach Bhan
Craig Veann
711
Drum na Clachh
Corrie of Allt nan Aighean
15
616
Geal Charn
16
Dalestie
17
18
19
The Fas
20
Corrie of Creag Mheann
585
10
Drum Bhuidh
2
Cnap Chaochan Aitinn
715
698
625
628
Cam Bhd a' Ghuail
Feith Bhait
09
Foal's Crag
Big Garvoun
742
Glen Loin
chrory

MAP 17

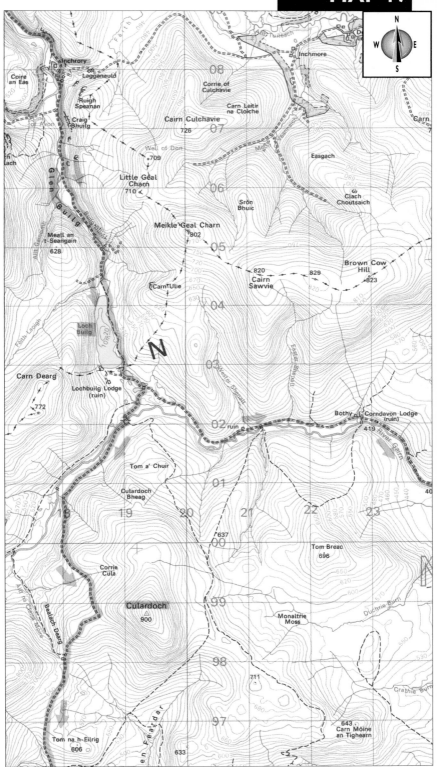

INVERCAULD HOUSE

BRAEMAR

Keep SO (S) for 2.3m (3.7km) – on obvious track into forest keeping L at T-junction at 1m (1.6km) – to X-roads just after gate. Go SO (SSW) for 0.3m (0.5km) – through R hairpin bend – to T-junction with Invercauld driveway. Take hairpin turn L (SE) for 1.1m (1.8km) to T-junction with unclassified county road by Keiloch Sawmill.

NOTE: for overnight in Braemar go SO to A93 then turn L for 3.25m (5.2km) to Braemar.

FELAGIE

BALMORAL

Turn L (NE) for 2.5m (4km) – passing Felagie and alongside forest – to T-junction then keep R (E) for 1.4m (2.2km) to A93 at Inver. Turn L (NE) for 2.4m (3.8km) to T-junction with B976 by Balmoral car-park (toilets here) then turn R (WSW then SE) for 8.25m (13.2km) – over River Dee – to T-junction at Ballater (**recommended 5th night**) and turn L (NW) over bridge 0.25m (0.4km) to Station Square.

BIKE CARE

Broken gear cables

● You'll be left with a granny ring (front) or small sprocket (rear). Use the high/low adjusters to shift the mechanism to a middle gear

Split tyre

● Usually caused by a rubbing brake block. Stop at once. Deflate and remove tyre bead from the rim on the damaged side. Place a bank note (Scotland has a wide variety) behind the split on the inside of the tyre with a margin folded over the bead of the tyre so it will be wedged against the rim when the tube's re-inflated. Pump up and ride carefully

DAY 6 Maps 19 – 23

BALLATER TO EDZELL
39m (62km), 22m (35km) off-road; 2850ft/865m climbing.
Summits and passes: Belrorie 775ft (235m); Mount Keen 2525ft (765m).

All the Coast-to-Coast off-road is wrapped up today – sob! Those with a mind to taste salt on the wind still with an adrenaline flutter in their hearts will have to dig deep into their fitness reserves to push for the final 15 road miles (24km) to Montrose.

Warm up and ride out along the scenic rail path that delivers you to Dinnet and by then your legs are supple enough to struggle over the ridge that divides Dinnet from Glen Tanar. Take a look round the Visitor Centre before gliding along the sandy tracks of Glen Tanar where once again majestic pines and – if it's fine – dancing shadows enhance the delights of summertime dirt-tracking. Out of the pines and up ahead looms Mount Keen – Scotland's easternmost Munro.

Once across the Water of Tanar it's instant granny-cog mode on a twisting, grit-spitting technical climb that will have you walking one way or another. Laden and that'll be on the first bends, riding light and in superhero mood you might make the 400m contour. Time to shoulder the frameset, put one foot in front of the other and wait for the grouse butts to show up (they're an ideal spot to take ten before mounting up – the next 3 miles (5km) are magic; they're also that last off-roading of the trip.).

If you're keen to bag a Munro then stash the bikes and follow the main pathway up to the summit and back. It's about a half-hour round trip. Now you're to be treated to sensuous singletracking as the Mounth Road contours round Mount Keen's boulder-strewn shoulder. The best is saved 'til last. But beware this twisting track descent; it's a bit of a snake with a few twists and turns that'll send you spinning into space if you don't take care! And watch out for walkers – cut that speed or you'll intimidate our fellow hill-goers. It finales in an unrideable ford – you have been warned!

The final run down to Edzell is along the delightful Glen Esk road but beware of traffic – it won't be expecting you. And don't be mislead by the Rights of Way signpost 'Lethnot and Brechin' and hang a right at the Dalbrack junction. We did, but the obvious cart track all the way down the far side of the beautiful North Esk valley passes through an estate that doesn't welcome cyclists – just walkers and horses.

MAP 18

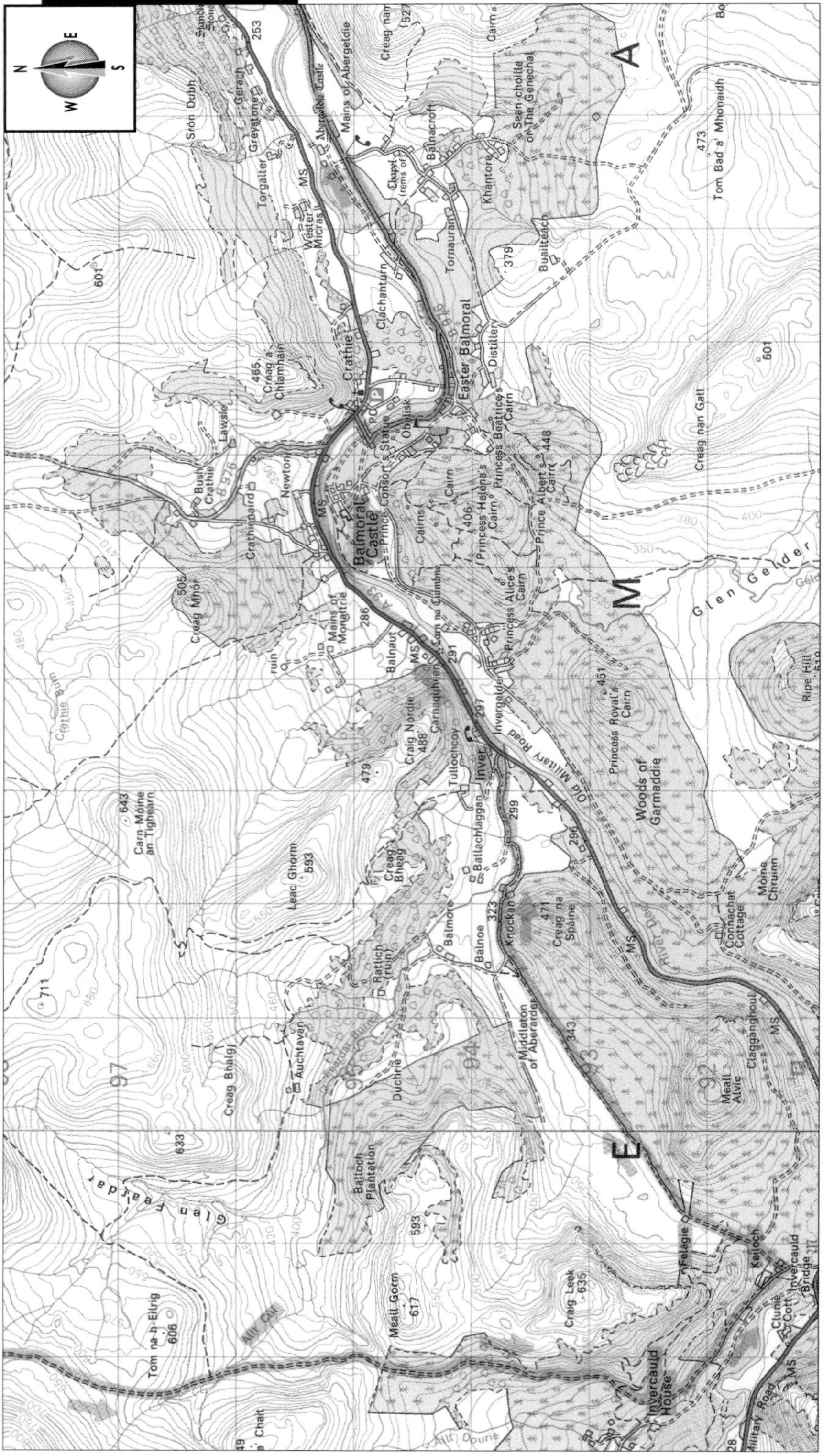

Balmoral Castle
Crathie
Easter Balmoral
Distillery
Abergeldie Castle
Mains of Abergeldie
Balnacroft
Khantore
Tornauran
Clachanturn
Wester Micras
Torgalter
Greystone
Sron Dubh
Sean-choille of The Genechal
Buailteach
Creag a Chlamhain
Lawsie
Newton
Bush Crathie
Crathienaird
Creag Mhor
Mains of Monaltrie
Balnault
Carnaquheen
Craig Nordie
Tullochcoy
Inver
Invergelder
Old Military Road
Princess Royal's Cairn
Woods of Garmaddie
Glen Gelder
Ripe Hill
Creag nan Gall
Tom Bad a' Mhonaidh
Ballachlaggan
Creag Bheag
Balmore
Balnoe
Knockan
Creag na Spaine
Duchrie
Middleton of Aberarder
Auchtavan
Creag Bhalgi
Leac Ghorm
Carn Moine an Tighearn
Glen Feardar
Tom na h-Eilrig
Meall Gorm
Craig Leek
Balloch Plantation
Felagie
Keiloch
Invercauld Bridge
Invercauld House
Meall Alvie
Connachat Cottage
Moine Chruinn
River Dee
Allt Dourie

MAP 19

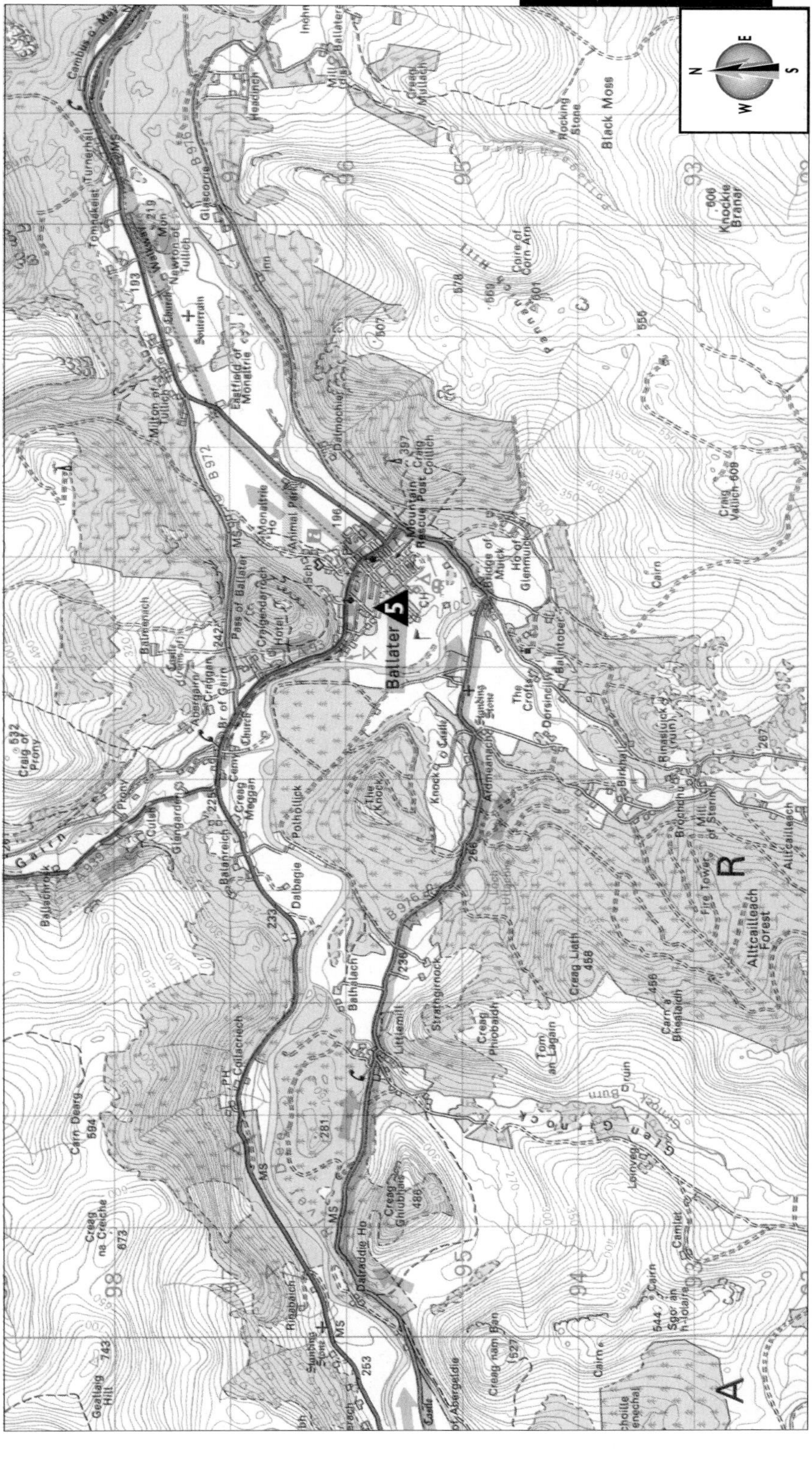

N
E
S
W
Ballater
5
Bridge of Muick
Ho of Glenmuick
Mountain Rescue Post
Craig Coillich
397
Monaltrie Ho
Animal Park
Pass of Ballater
Craigendarroch
Hotel
Craggan
Abergairn
Br of Gairn
Balmenach
Craig of Prony
532
Prony
Culsh
Glengarden
Balanreich
Creag Meggen
Pollhollick
Dalbagie
The Knock
Knock o' Castle
Standing Stone
Ardmeanach
The Crofts
Dorsincilly
Balintober
Birkhall
Brochdhu
Mill of Sterin
Fire Tower
Alltcailleach Forest
Alltcailleach
Creag Liath
458
Strathgirnock
Creag Phiobaidh
Tom an Lagain
Littlemill
Bathalach
Craig Vallich
608
Coire of Corn Arn
Black Moss
Rocking Stone
Knockie Branar
606
Creag Mullach
Headinch
Glascorrie
Inn
Newton of Tullich
Tomnakeist
Turnerhall
Cambus o' May
Milton of Tullich
Eastfield of Monaltrie
Dalmochie
B 972
B 976
Dee
Coilacriech
Carn Dearg
594
Creag na Creiche
673
Geallaig Hill
743
Rinabaich
Standing Stone
Dalraddie Ho
Creag Ghiubhais
486
Creag nam Ban
527
Glen Girnock
Loinveg
Sgor an h-Iolaire
544
A
R

BALLATER From Station Square join the Cambus o'May Walkway (it follows a disused railway and is clearly signed) (NE) for 7m (11km) – take care crossing the A93 – to Dinnet. Turn R (SSE) for 0.15m (0.25km) on B9119 to T-junction with B976 then turn L (E) for 0.8m (1.2km) to T-junction with

DINNET SCHOOL track opposite Dinnet School then turn R (SSE) for 0.6m (1km) – forking R at T-junction at 0.25m (0.4km) – up to T-junction. Turn L (SE) for 0.9m (1.3km) – soon to join tarmac drive – to T-

MILLFIELD junction with C-road in Millfield then fork R (W) for 0.1m (0.15km) to X-roads with track (car park off R). Zigzag L/R (SW) for 0.5m (0.8km) –

GLEN TANAR VISITOR CENTRE immediately crossing Bridge of Tanar, with Glen Tanar Visitor Centre and toilets to your L, then on track past chapel – to T-junction. Turn R (SW then S) for 0.5m (0.8km) – turning R at staggered X-roads at 0.12m (0.2km) – to Knockie Bridge signed 'Glen Esk'.

GLEN TANAR Zigzag R/L (S) over bridge and for 4.5m (7.2km) – up Glen Tanar on obvious track, out of forest and keeping L at T-junction at 4m (6.4km) – to T-junction then fork L (SE) for 1.5m (2.4km) – over two bridges – to signed track X-roads. Fork L (S) for 0.8m (1.2km) – on obvious Mounth Road track, over footbridge then up steep climb – to X-roads

MOUNTH ROAD with singletrack off L and vague track off R. Keep SO (SSE) for 0.6m (1km) – a carry up rubbly singletrack – to T-junction with minor singletrack (main singletrack heads SSE for summit of Mount Keen) beyond grouse butts then fork R (SSW) for 1.7m (2.7km) – following small cairns round shoulder of

MOUNT KEEN Mount Keen – to T-junction with shooting track.

Fork L (SE) for 1.7m (2.7km) – down obvious track and watch out for drainage barriers and

LADDER BURN Ladder Burn zigzags! – to Glenmark fords (Deep!). Keep SO (S) for 2.6m (4.2km) – down Glen Mark

GLEN ESK – to T-junction with C-road in Glen Esk (**accommodation available**), then turn L (E) for 13m (21km) to T-junction with B966 (alternative route dotted on maps 22–23) then turn R (S) for 1.5m (2.4km) to Edzell (**accommodation available – recommended 6th night**).

The picturesque Glen Esk road, the final leg of the journey on the way to Edzell.

BIKE CARE

Totalled rear mechanism

● Split the chain and remove the mech entirely. Put the chain round the middle chainring and a middle sprocket. Rejoin it, discarding sufficient links to take up slack, and you'll have a single-speed clunker

Loose headset

● Use a toe strap or zip-tie tightened on the race to take out any play – turn it clockwise – then repeat the procedure on the locknut

---

MAP 20

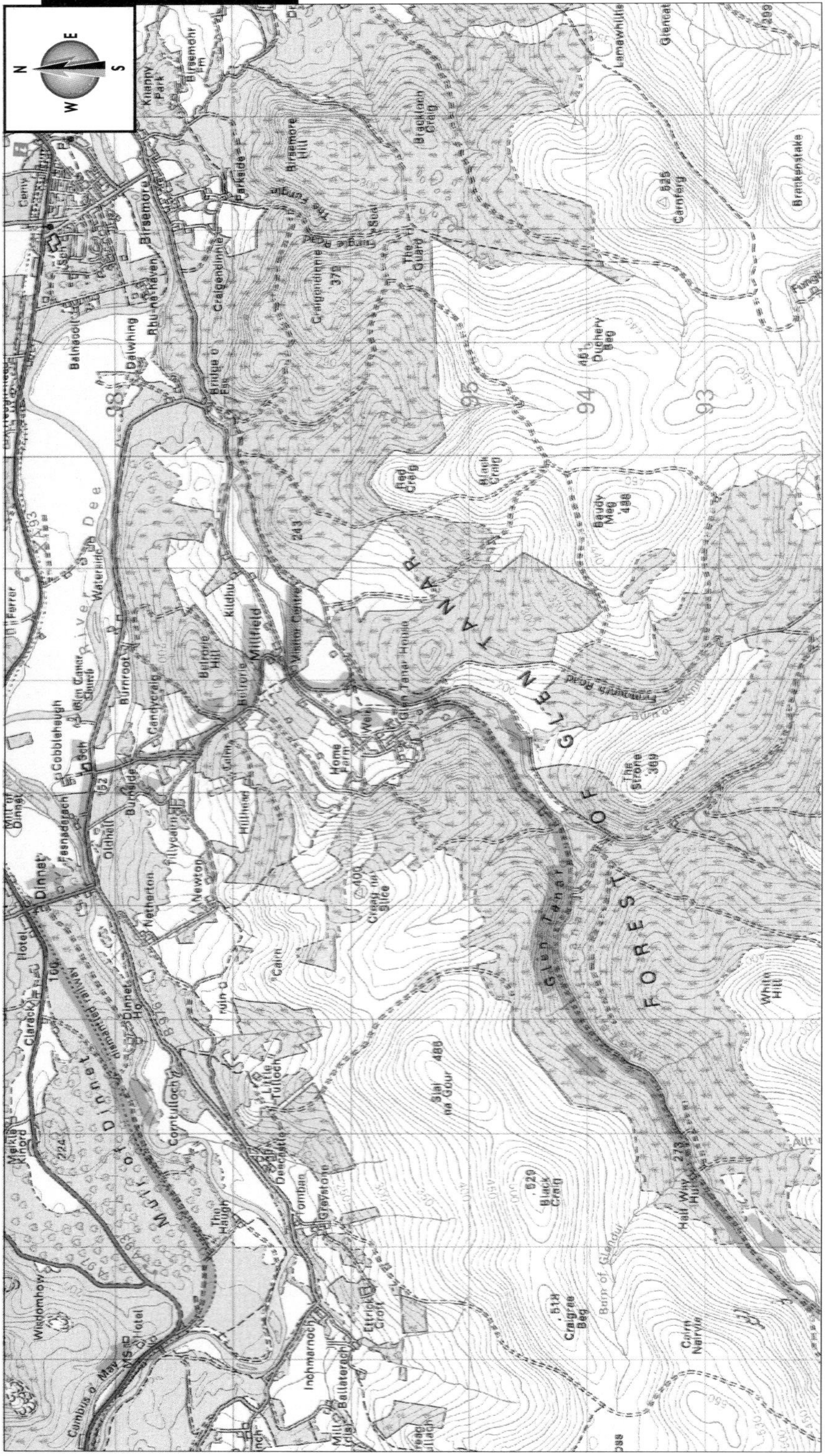

N E S W

Knapny Park
Birsemohr Fm
Braemohr
Braemore Fm
Braemore Hill
Brackloch Craig
Birsemore
Parkside
Lamawhillie
Glenat
Carnferg
Brakenstake
Funeroad
Balnacraig
Rhu-na-haven
Dalwhing
Craigendinnie
Burnt Seat
Burnt Wood
The Guard
Dinnery Bog
Balnagowff
Craigendinnie
Bridge o'Ess
River Dee
Waterside
FOREST OF GLEN TANAR
Red Craig
Black Craig
Baudy Meg
Glen Tanar Sheil
Birrroot
Kildhu
Visitor Centre
Millfield
Belrorie Hill
Candycraig
Glen Tanar House
Firmounth Road
Cobbleheugh
Bucheat
Cairn
Home Farm
Oldhell
Pannanich
Hillhead
Tillyearn
The Stone
Newton
Netherton
Craig nd Slde
Cairn
Mill of Dinnet
Dinnet
Hotel
Clarack Burn
Tilquhillie
Dinnet Ho
ruin o
Cairn
FOREST OF
White Hill
Little Tulloch
Slol na Gour
MUIR OF DINNET
Cortulloch
Descalde
Half Way Hut
Tomhan
Cromian
Treyshohn
Black Craig
Burn of Glendui
Wester Knowd
Craigree Beg
Cairn Narryn
Wiedomtowr
The Haugh
Inchmarnock
Cambus o' May Hotel
Milton of Ballaterich

MAP 21

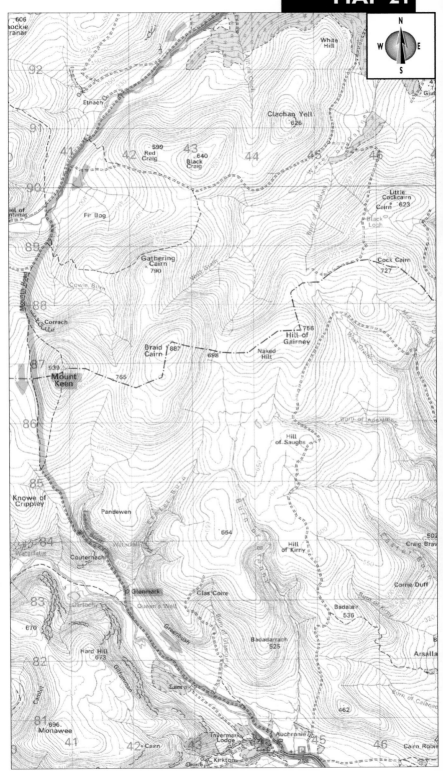

The Ladder descent at Mount Keen. Take it carefully, or its twists and turns may take their toll on you!

DAY 7 Maps 23 – 24

EDZELL TO THE NORTH SEA (MONTROSE)
15m (24km), no off-road cycling; 500ft (155m) climbing.
Summits and passes: Hill of Stracathro 390ft/119m.

It's ambletime all the way to Montrose. Not a pretty town, but the beach is definitely the North Sea and the breezes have the tang of salt last tasted when you put the Isle of Skye at your back seven days ago!

EDZELL	Go SO (SSE) for 2m (3.2km) – towards Brechin on B966, under A94 – to T-junction then turn L (NE) for 3.7m (6km) – keeping SO at T-junction off R
HILLSIDE	to Dun at 1m (1.6km) – to A937 at Hillside. Turn R (SSE) for 1m (1.6km) – towards Montrose town centre – to T-junction with A92 then go SO (S) 1m (1.6km) – keeping SO at T-junction with A935 and past chapel on your L – to T-junction with minor road signed 'Beach'. Turn L (E) 0.8m
MONTROSE BAY	(1.2km) – past golf links club house – to Montrose Bay beach. Go dip your tyres in the North Sea!

OFF-ROAD CODE
● Do not race
● Keep erosion to a minimum and do not skid
● Be courteous and considerate to others

The serene Glen Avon river winds its way through the Grampians.

MAP 22

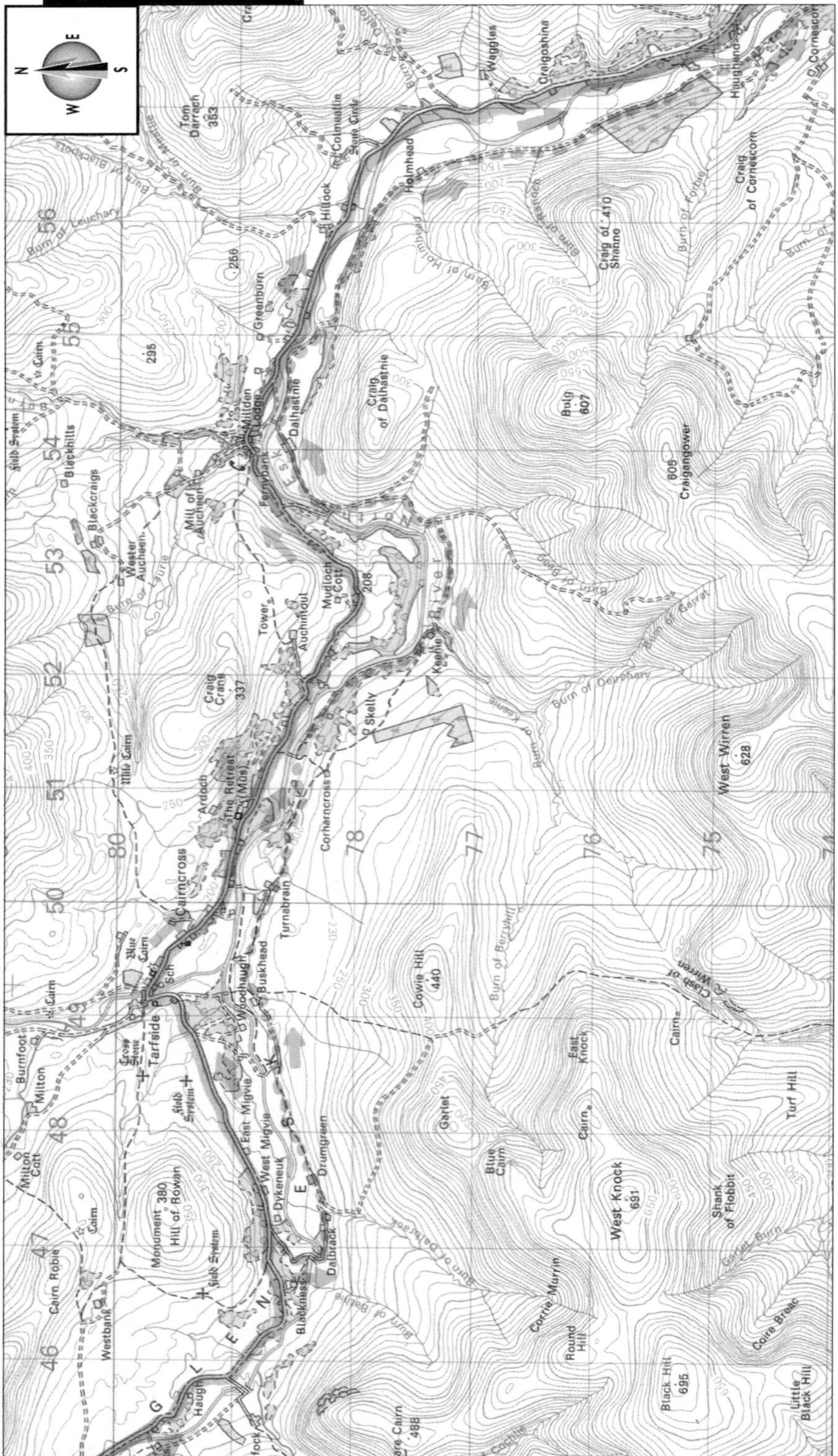

N
E
W
S

Burn of Leuchary

Tom of Darrach
353

Burn of King

Blackwalls

Craig

Waggles
Craigophine

Cornescorn

Craig of Cornescorn

Burn of Forbes

Hillock

Colpnottie

Scots Girth

Helmhead

56

Greenburn

295

Milldin

256

Blackhills

Blackcraig

54

Wester Auchern

Mill of Auchert

Dalhaitnie

53

Tower

Mudloch or Cott

208

Craig of Dalhaitnie

Bridg
607

Craigangowver

Burn of Garral

Auchinlout

52

Craig Crang
337

Kepho

Skellv

West Wirren
628

Burn of Ogreshary

Little Cairn

51

Burn of Berryhill

80

Ardoch
The Retreat
(Mos)

Corharncross

78

77

76

75

Cairncross

50

Turnabrain

Blue Cairn

Sch

Cowie Hill
440

Chash of W Wirren

N. Cairn

49

Buskhead

Woodaught

Tarfside

Burnfoot

Milton

Cross Stone

East Migvie

Garlet

East Knock

Cairns

Turf Hill

48

Milton Cott

Slab System

West Migvie

Dykeneuk

Drumgreen

Cairn

Blue Cairn

West Knock
691

Shank of Fiddbt

Cairn Robie

47

Monument 380
Hill of Rowan

Dalbrack

Burn of Dalbrack

Corrie Murrin

Care Braes

Westbank

Slab System

Blackhaugh

Round Hill

Black Hill
695

Little Black Hill

46

Hare Cairn
398

Burn of Cochie

Haugh

Burn of Tennet

MAP 23

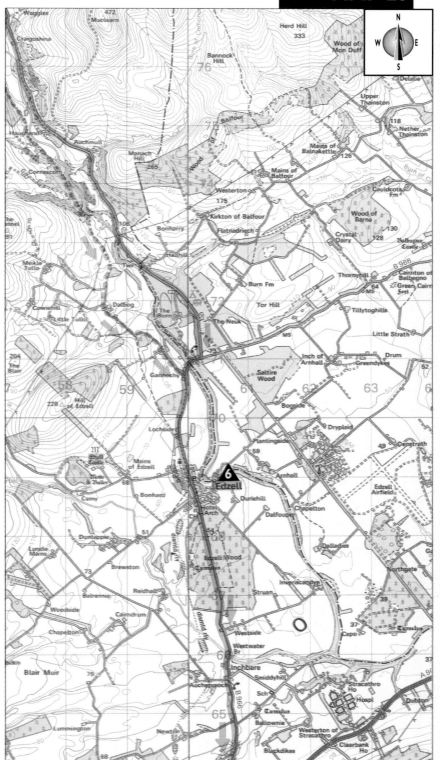

MAP 24

N E S W

Links of Montrose
Dunes
Rathhead
Commieston
Stracatho 52
Stone of
Morphie
Den
Kinnaber
Woodfield
Cott
Charleton
Distillery
Mill of
Morphie
Weir
Maines of
Logie
Church
Logie
Canterland
Forebank
35
Logie Mill
53
Craigo
52
Denhead
Cotts
Loop
Dubton
Mains of
Hedderwick
Barrewfield
A 935
Cemy
Rosemount
Craigo
Sch
North
Craigo
Mulraside
of Craigo
Broomley
South Hill
Home Fm
Hillhead of
Hedderwick
97
West Mains of
Hedderwick
Langley
Park
Kirkhill
Welthill
Pugeston
Newbigging Fm
Tayock
Cemy
Montrose
Ardoch
44
Logie Pert
North Hill
of Craigo
Bank of
Gallery
Glenskinno
Wood
Glen-Wood
Glenskinno
Fordhouse
House of Dun
Glenley
Broomley
Bridge of Dun
Drum
69
75
Glen of
Craigo
107
112
Balloohy
North Mains
of Dun
North Dun
66
Dun
Mains of
Dun
61
Batwyllo
Muir of Pert
86
Murton
of Balloohy
98
111
Damside
Dun's
Dish
Woodside
of Balnillo
65
Leys of Dun
Balnillo
A 935
Arrat's Mill
Whitfield
of Dun
Addiclate
Leightonhill
Caldcots
64
Leuchland
Plantation
Windyedge
Arrat
19
Kincraig
28
Balbirnie
Mill
Hill of
Stracatho
119
Huntlyhill
101
63
Caledonian Rly
Kinnaide Mill
Westeston of
Stracatho
Clearbank
Ho
Stone
1452
South
Ardo
106
62
Leuchland
81
37
Weir
Coldhill
Dalgety
52
Ballownie
Blackdikes
Newtonmill
Syde
Templewood
Wardhill
Tillygloom
87
East
Pitforthie
62
Sewage
Wks
99
East Mains
of Keithock
Trinity
88
Mains of
Pitforthie
61
Glencadam
Ho
Drumachie
Keithock
Little
Keithock
Unthank

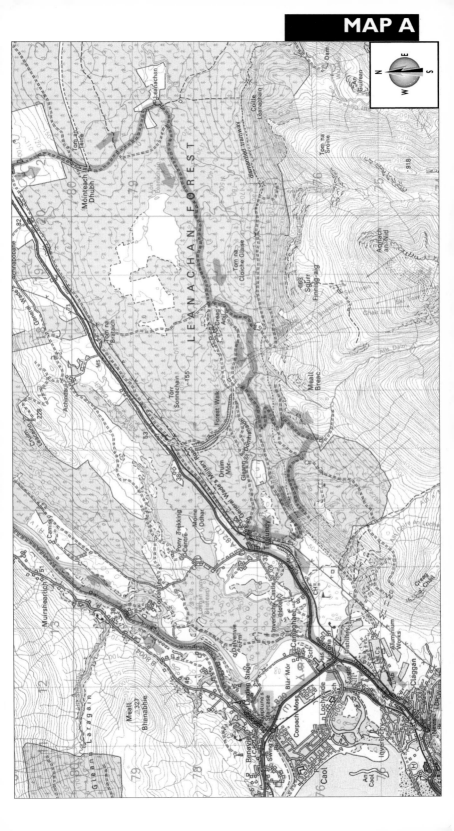

MAP A

DAY RIDES ON THE HIGHLAND COAST-TO-COAST TRAIL

The following three day rides are all circular tours which can either be added to the main route, or completed as seperate tours in themselves. The maps for these day rides follow in the next few pages.

Leanachan Forest and Caledonian Canal [Maps A – B]

Distance: 25 miles (40km); 1800ft climbs.
Time: 3hrs (dry), 3.5hrs (wet).
Grade: Easy/moderate.
An easy-going, low level loop that kicks off with a climb up Neptune's Staircase for a cruise alongside the Caledonian Canal. Away to your right the Nevis Range sweeps down into Leanachan Forest where you'll meet a heady mix of fast, forest fire road interleaved with demanding singletrack, once featured in a British Mountain Biking race circuit.

LOCATION	ROUTE DIRECTIONS
FORT WILLIAM	Start at Nevis Bridge roundabout, Fort·William (GR113743) turn L (NE) on A82 for 1.25m (1.15km) to T-junction with traffic lights then turn L (NW) on A830 for 1m (1.6km) – following Great Glen Cycle Route – then turn R then almost immediately L (NE, signed GGCR) for 6.4m (10.2km) – up onto Caledonian Canal towpath to
GAIRLOCHY	gate at Gairlochy (café here) – to B8004.
SPEAN BRIDGE	Turn R (ENE) for 2.5m (4km) to T-junction with A82 (Commando Memorial here) then fork R (SE, Fort William) for 2m (3.2km) – through Spean Bridge – to X-roads then turn L (SSE, signed 'Leanachan') for 2m (3.2km) – past barrier at

Leanachan House – to track T-junction then fork R (SW) for 0.6m (1km) to T-junction then fork L (WSW) over bridge for 1.6m (2.6km) to go through gate on X-roads.

Turn L (SSW) for 0.2m (0.3km) to T-junction then turn L (SW) to climb for 0.5m (0.8km) to T-junction (Waymarker 'Arrow' indicates BMB race course) then turn R (NW) for 0.8m (1.3km) – onto vague track (boggy when wet) but obvious, meandering singletrack – to forest track.

Turn R (NE) for Gondola Station tea shop, otherwise turn L (WSW) for 0.4m (0.6km) to T-junction then turn L (SSW then SE) for 0.75m (1.2km) – round hairpin bend – to 'End of Cycle Route'. Turn R (WNW) for 0.4m (0.6km) – down twisting singletrack (watch rock step 25yds/25m after ford) – to T-junction with old tram route then turn L (W) 110yds (100m) to forest track.

TORLUNDY Turn R (NNE) for 0.2m (0.3km) down to T-junction. Turn L (NW) for 0.7m (1.15km) – along contouring track – to T-junction then turn R (NW) for 0.12m (0.2km) down to junction then turn L (SW then NW then N) for 0.8m (1.3km) – following fence line then pylons – down to C-road at Torlundy. Turn L (W) for 0.2m (0.3km) to T-junction with A82. Turn L (S) for 3m (4.8km) – keeping SO at traffic lights – to start.

OFF-ROAD CODE
● **Be self-sufficient and make sure your bike is safe to ride**
● **Wear a helmet**

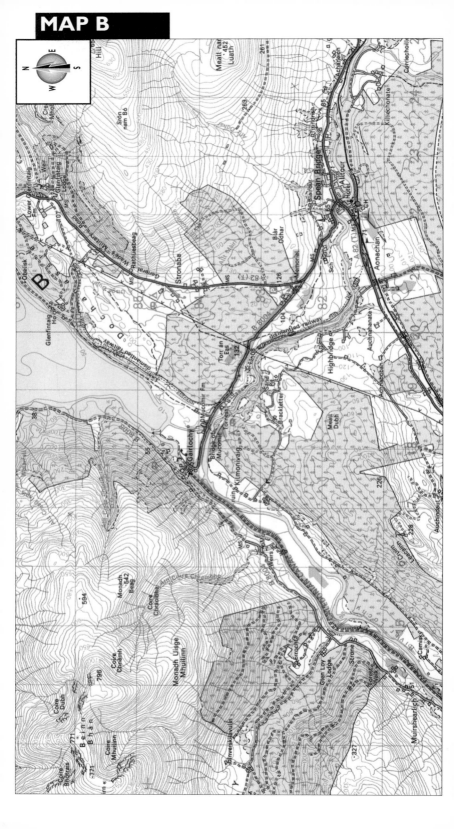

MAP B

MAP C

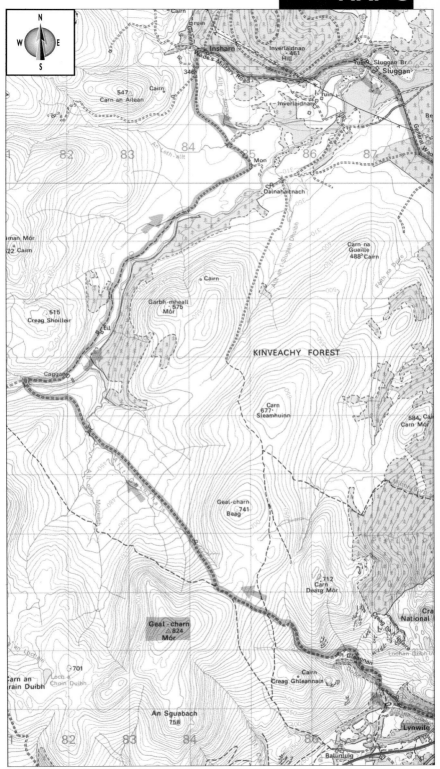

Aviemore/East Shoulder of Geal-charn Mór and the River Dulnain [Maps C & D]

Distance: 20m (32km), 13m (20.8km) off-road.
Ascent: 2000ft (610m).
Time: 4–5 hours.
Grade: Moderate/difficult.

A route with a real mountain feel to it. A loop running from the Spey Valley to the north-west over the Mandhliath Mountains and finishing in Aviemore. Ideal for the aspiring climber and downhill specialist.

The route starts in Aviemore and takes the long, tough climb over the east shoulder of Geal-charn Mór. The views to the east of the skiing and climbing corries of Cairngorm are magnificent. The long, glaciated glens of Feshie, Einich and the Lairig Ghru are seen to their best advantage.

On reaching the summit you are in grouse country, evident by the grouse butts on the high moor. It is a place not to linger in cold or threatening weather, as there is no shelter. At around 2200ft (670m) the wind-chill can be extremely high on a windy day.

The descent to the River Dulnain is long and fast on a wide track, originally an old drove route.

The grassy track along the west side of the river is relatively smooth. A peaceful and relaxing glen to enjoy with a couple of small fords in the stream to negotiate.

Here the track is more obvious and links up with the old General Wade military road at Sluggan Bridge. The old military road is now followed along the side of the Beananach Wood to Speyside and your return to Aviemore.

AVIEMORE	Leave rail station in Aviemore and travel S on B9152 for 1.2m (2km) and cross A9 to Lynwilg.
GEAL CHARN MÓR **INSHARN**	Now climb the track leading (NW) to the E shoulder of Geal-charn Mór. Descend to the bridge at GR813165. turn R and follow track (NE) along the river Dulnain, crossing two small fords. Turn L (NNW) at Monument (climb gate), 1.6m (2.5km) to Insharn. Turn R (E) to Sluggan Bridge 1.9m (3km).

GENERAL WADE MILITARY ROAD

ALLT LORGY

Continue SSE on General Wade Military Road along edge of Beananach Wood for 1.2m (2km). Turn L and just past X-roads after 280yds (250m) turn R. Cross ford on Allt Lorgy to cattle grid after 0.9m (1.5km). 0.6m (1km) to Y-junction and turn L.

Turn L (N) at T-junction to main junction on A9. Proceed with caution across A9 and railway. Turn R (SE) on B9153 the 4.4m (7km) to finish at Aviemore.

AVIEMORE

The Cairngorm mountains are always a striking sight, even from many miles away.

MAP D

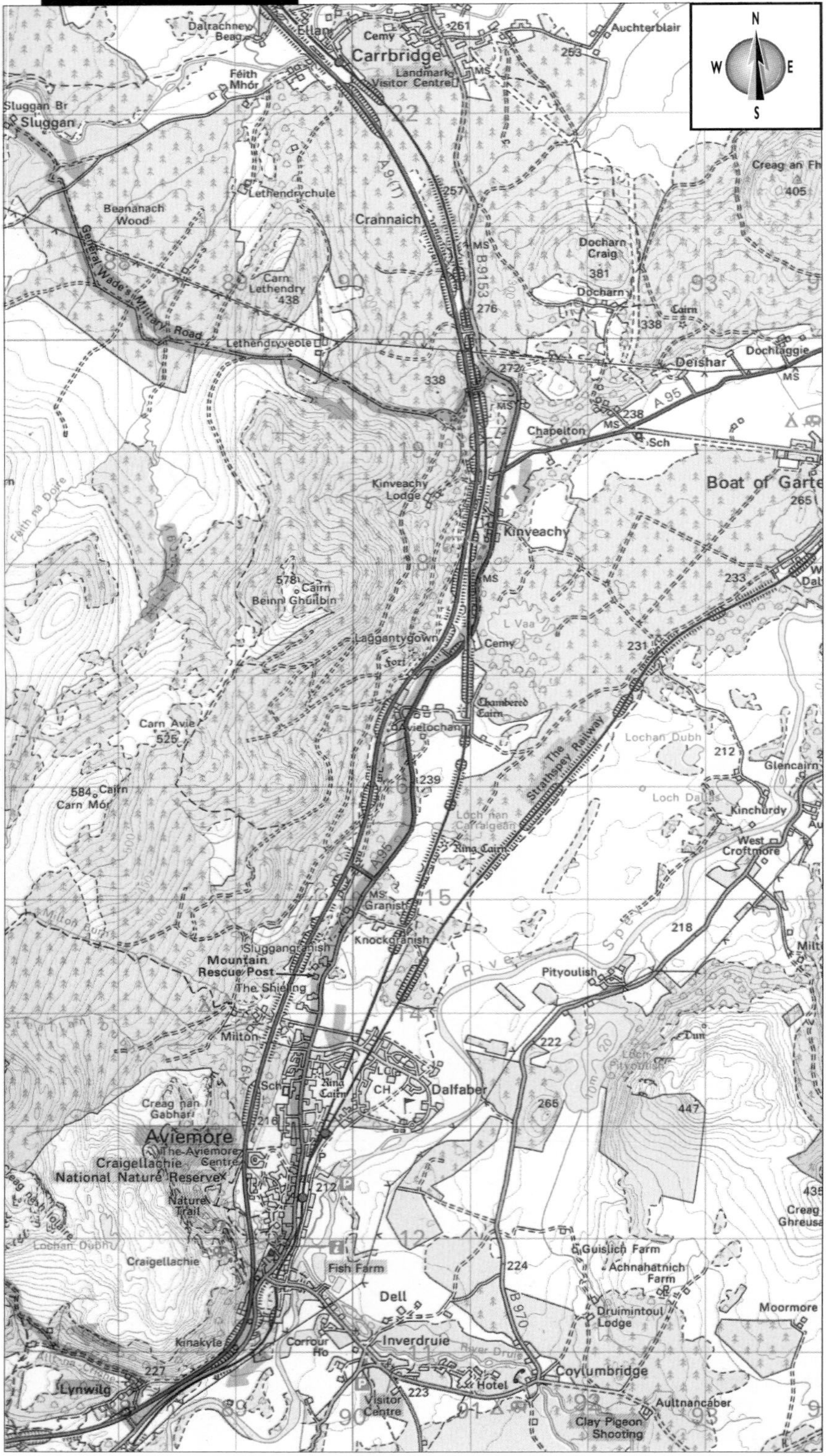
N
S
E
W
Dalrachney Beag
Ellan
Cemy
Carrbridge
261
Auchterblair
253
Landmark Visitor Centre
MS
Fèith Mhór
Sluggan Br
Sluggan
22
Creag an Fh
405
A9(T)
257
Lethendrychule
Beananach Wood
Crannaich
MS
B9153
Docharn Craig
381
General Wade's Military Road
Carn Lethendry
438
90
276
Docharn
93
Cairn
338
Lethendryveole
20
272
Deishar
Dochlaggie
MS
338
MS
A 95
238
MS
Chapelton
Sch
19
Boat of Garte
265
Kinveachy Lodge
Kinveachy
MS
233
578
Cairn
Beinn Ghuilbin
L Vaa
Laggantygown
Cemy
231
Fort
Chambered Cairn
Avielochan
Carn Avie
525
The Strathspey Railway
Lochan Dubh
212
Glencairn
239
584
Cairn
Carn Mór
Loch Dallas
Kinchurdy
Loch nan Carraigean
Ring Cairn
West Croftmore
A95
MS
Granish
15
218
Knockgranish
Sluggangranish
Mountain Rescue Post
The Shieling
River Spey
Pityoulish
14
Milton
222
Dun
Loch Pityoulish
A9(T)
Sch
Ring Cairn
CH
Dalfaber
265
447
Creag nan Gabhar
216
Aviemore
The Aviemore Centre
Craigellachie National Nature Reserve
212
Nature Trail
435
Creag Ghreusa
Lochan Dubh
12
Craigellachie
Fish Farm
224
Guislich Farm
Achnahatnich Farm
Dell
B 970
Druimintoul Lodge
Moormore
Kinakyle
Corrour Ho
Inverdruie
River Druie
227
Coylumbridge
Lynwilg
223
Hotel
Aultnancaber
Visitor Centre
89
90
91
92
93
Clay Pigeon Shooting

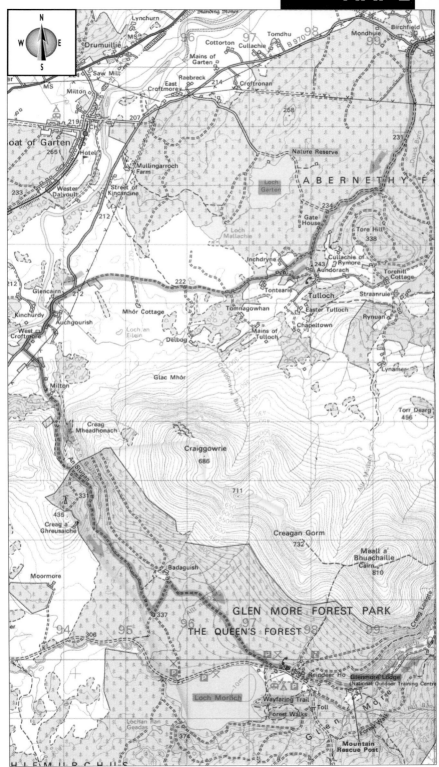

Ryvoan Pass and the Slugan Pass [Maps E & F]

Distance: 20m (32km), 12m (19km) off-road.
Ascent: 1000ft (305m).
Time: 4–5 hours.
Grade: Easy/moderate.

A superb circuit looping off the Highland Coast-to-coast route near Forest Lodge in the Abernethy Forest. A route considered to be one of the finest introductions to mountain-biking in the area, equally suitable to the novice or experienced mountain-biker.

The route starts at Loch Morlich and passes through the Abernethy Forest, which is now owned and cared for by the Royal Society for the Protection of Birds (RSPB). For those intersted in the wildlife, this is an excellent opportunity to observe some of the rare birds and animals peculiar to the ancient Caledonian Pine Forest.

This is a route of ever-changing panoramic views and time should be taken to enjoy them. The climb up through the Ryvoan Pass is gradual, and on looking south near Lochan Uaine (The Green Loch), the high tops of the Cairngorms can be pinpointed. The path seen winding in the distance through the Chalamain Gap leads to the Lairig Ghru, the highest pass in Scotland.

On passing Ryvoan Bothy a few undulations lead you into the long gradual descent to Nethy Bridge. A series of fast forest tracks lead eventually onto surfaced road at Dell Lodge. Nethy Bridge has all the refreshments necessary and bike hire is available if required. The return via the Slugan Pass is initially on surfaced roads past the RSPB osprey reserve at Loch Garten. When turning off at the Milton Burn to start the final off-road section to the top of the pass, a terrific view north is your just reward. The tracks down to Loch Morlich and the finish are wide and in good order making it a relaxing end to the day.

LOCH MORLICH	Leave car park at café opposite Loch Morlich Youth Hostel. Turn R (SSE) for 0.2m (0.3km) along ski road towards Cairngorm. Turn L (E) to start gradual ascent to Ryvoan, surfaced road to
GLENMORE LODGE	Glenmore Lodge. Continue on forest track (NNE) to An Lochan Uaine 1.3m (2km) from Glenmore Lodge. Shortly after, the track narrows and turns
RYVOAN BOTHY	rocky. At junction to Bynack Stables bear L to Ryvoan Bothy.

The track surface improves now and continues generally N to edge of wood and start of descent towards Forest Lodge. 0.6m (1km) from edge of wood turn L at Y-junction. Take hairpin bend R and climb out of forest crossing the Allt Clais nan Caorach.

FOREST LODGE

Continue for 110yds (100m) to junction at the edge of wood. Continue R (E) for 0.2m (0.3km) to Y-junction. Turn L (N) down the west side of the River Nethy to X-roads. Continue N for 110yds (100m) to T-junction. Turn L (W) at T-junction for 0.4m (0.6km) to point 294m. Turn R (N).

NETHY BRIDGE

LOCH GARTEN

Continue N for 1.8m (3km) to the start of surfaced road near Dell Lodge. At Nethy Bridge turn L (W) for 0.3m (0.5km) on B970 towards Coylumbridge. Turn L (S) for 2.2m (3.5km) on road to Loch Garten. At junction to Loch Garten continue SSW. Turn R (W) at Klondyke Cottage to T-junction on B970. Turn L (SSW) and continue for 0.6m (1km). Turn L (SE) at edge of wood. Follow track past Kincardine Cottage to gate where the climb to the top of Slugan Pass starts. The cattle grid after 0.9m (1.5km) at the edge of the forestry marks the outstanding viewpoint N.

LOCH MORLICH

Continue for 1.2m (2km) to X-roads at point 337m (GR954108). Turn L (NNE) for 0.3m (0.5km) to T-junction. Turn R (SSE) for 275yds (250m) to T-junction. Turn R (E) for 0.2m (0.3km) to bend where track turns SE towards Loch Morlich. Ignore all junctions from both sides to emerge at the ski road and SYHA Hostel entrance opposite the café start point.

 OFF-ROAD CODE
- **Follow a route marked on a map**
- **Follow the Country Code**

Nethy Bridge
Birchfield
Hotel
Blairgorm
D Garlyne
Sliemore
04
02
299
Lower Dell
Lynstock
Ellaneorn
247
238
Dell Lodge
Lettoch
318
Laggandhu
19
231
Laintachan
327
Lainc
252
Clachaig
Balno
THY FOREST
18
Ailanbeg
Knockailan
Attinlea
Laintachan
Dorback Burn
17
Lurg
310
Torebill Cottage
263
Lyngarrie
325
Loch an Spioraid
Cuchanlupe
16
294
Forest Lodge
Carr
nruie
Bognacruie
Cairn Rynettin
472
ruin
Carn a' Chnuic
505
Lynamer
Rynettin
Torr Dearg
456
Ford
Loch a' Chnuic
14
Memorial
13
12
Carn Bheadhair
803
Ryvoan Bothy
ll a'
haille
310
Loch a'
Garbh-choire
Allt Bheadhair
11
Creag Loisgte
ARK
Nature Reserve
Lochan Uaine
Bynack Stable
03
04
05
Creag nan Gall
622
Allt Fonn a' Choire
01
Lodge
Outdoor Training Centre
Mam Suim
An Lurg
753
Stac na h-Iolaire
742
692
737
Lochan
na Beinne
919

APPENDICES

The following pages are a directory of useful contacts for Highland Coast-to-Coasters including hostels, bike shops, Forest Enterprise, Scot Rail and Tourist Information offices.

Weather News
Western Highlands
☎ 0891 500 441
☎ 0891 500 425
Grampians
☎ 0891 500 442
☎ 0891 500 424

Tourist Information Centres
Kyle of Lochalsh
☎ 01599 534276
Inverness
☎ 01463 234353
Fort William
☎ 01397 703781
Aviemore
☎ 01479 810363
Glen More Centre
☎ 01479 861220
Tomintoul
☎ 01807 580285
Braemar
☎ 013397 41600
Ballater
☎ 013397 55306
Balmoral Estate
☎ 013397 42334
Brechin
☎ 01356 623050
Montrose
☎ 01674 672000

Scottish Youth Hostels
SYHA National Office
7 Glebe Crescent
Stirling FK8 2JA

☎ 01786 451181
SYHAs en-route
Ratagan
☎ 0159981 243
Loch Lochy
☎ 01809 501239
Glen Nevis
☎ 01397 702336
Loch Morlich
☎ 01479 861238
Braemar
☎ 013397 41659

Private Hostels and Bunkhouses en-route
Tomdoun Hotel, Tomdoun
☎ 01809 511218/244
Abbey Backpackers Lodge, Fort Augustus
☎ 01320 366233
Aite Cruinnichidh Achluachrach, Glen Spean
☎ 01397 712315
The Grey Corrie Lodge, Roybridge
☎ 01397 712236
Craigellachie Lodge, Newtonmore
☎ 01540 673360
Kirkbeag Cabin, Kingussie
☎ 01540 651298
Glen Feshie Hostel, Balachoick, near Feshiebridge
☎ 01540 601323
Braemar Mountain Sports Bunkhouse,
The Mews, Braemar
☎ 013397 41242

Bike Shops and Bike Hire
Highland bike shops are not able to carry a huge amount of stock so you should telephone first to check if they have what you're looking for. Generally, they are all extremely helpful and if they are not able to solve your problem then you can always resort to 'Royal Mail Rescue'. How? Well, if you have a helpful local shop then pre-arrange for them to post urgently needed bits of kit by Royal Mail Special Delivery.
Off-Beat Bikes, MacRaes Lane, Fort William
☎ 01397 704008
Nevis Cycles (limited facilities), Spean Bridge
☎ 01397 712404
Inverdruie MTB Shop, Rothiemurchus Information Centre Inverdruie, near Aviemore
☎ 01479 810787
Speyside Sports Grampian Road, Aviemore
☎ 01479 810656
Sportshire, Nethy Bridge Abernethy
☎ 01479 821333
Bridge of Brown Tearoom Craft Shop, Tomintoul
☎ 01807 580335

Braemar Mountain Sports
The Mews, Braemar
☎ 013397 41242
Making Treks
Station Square, Ballater
☎ 013397 55865
BG Cycles
Aboyne Mart, Aboyne
☎ 013398 85355

Scot Rail Booking Information

Scotland
☎ 0345 212282 (Local rate)
Fort William
☎ 01397 703791
Inverness
☎ 01463 238924

Forest Enterprise

North Scotland Regional
Office, 21 Church Street
Inverness IV1 1EL
☎ 01463 232811
Lochaber District office,
Fort William
☎ 01397 702184
Fort Augustus
District office
☎ 01320 6322
Inverness District office
☎ 01463 791575
Kincardine District office,
Banchory
☎ 0133 044537
Tay District office, Dunkeld
☎ 01350 727284

Scottish Rights of Way Society

Since 1845, the Scottish
Rights of Way Society has
been safeguarding rights of
way for the benefit of the
public. They are not an
official body or
government department
but a charitable voluntary
group. Without their
dedication and effort many
of the routes we enjoy today – including much of
the Highland Coast–to-
Coast – would be denied
us.

In addition to
safeguarding Rights of
Way, the Society gives
advice on matters relating
to Rights of Way, secures
recognition of Rights of
Way and signposts major
routes. The best way that
you can help and show
your appreciation for their
work is by becoming a
member or by making a
donation. Their address
and telephone is:
Scottish Rights of Way
Society,
John Cotton Business
Centre,
10 Sunnyside,
Edinburgh EH7 5RA
☎ 0131 652 2937

The Cyclists Touring Club

Since 1878 the Cyclists
Touring Club (CTC) has
been the governing body
for recreational cycling in
this country and is recognised by such organisa-
tions as the Sports
Council, the Department
of Transport and the
Department of the
Environment.

Membership is open to
anyone interested in
cycling. They currently
have 40,000 members,
200 nation-wide clubs and
100 local clubs affiliated to
them.

Recently the CTC has
taken on responsibility for
addressing off-road cycling
access issues which
includes promoting Rights
of Way initiatives
wherever they occur and
representing the views of
mountain bikers at local
and national levels. Local
representation is done
through a network of
volunteer Access Officers.

If you would like to
apply for membership and
receive more information
then please apply to:
CTC
Dept CSB/94,
69 Meadrow,
Godalming,
Surrey GU7 3HS
☎ 01483 417217

Benefits of being a
member include: represen-
tation on Rights of Way
and access issues in your
area; third party insurance
cover; free legal advice for
cycling related problems;
free legal aid; free technical
advice; free international
touring info; bi-monthly
colour magazine; free
handbook; mail order
service; a voice in the
world of MTBing.